Being a DAD Is **WEIRD**

Being
a DAD Is
WEIRD

LESSONS IN FATHERHOOD
FROM MY FAMILY TO YOURS

BEN FALCONE

DEY ST.
An Imprint of WILLIAM MORROW

FIRST EDITION

Designed by Joy O'Meara

Library of Congress Cataloging-in-Publication Data has been applied for.

ISBN 978-0-06-247362-2

17 18 19 20 21   DIX/LSC   10 9 8 7 6 5 4 3 2 1

To my wonderful daughters, Vivian and Georgette—
thanks for teaching me so much.
To my lovely wife, Mooch—thanks for
sharing the fun of being a parent with me.
To my brother, my mom, and of course my pop—
thanks for everything. Much love to you all.

CONTENTS

_____

Contents

Contents

Contents

FOREWORD

WHEN BEN FIRST ASKED me to write the foreword for his book, my immediate response was, "You wrote a book? When did you have time to write a book?"

In typical Ben Falcone fashion, without any pomp or circumstance, he had secretly, quietly written a book.

I was, of course, honored and excited to write the foreword to my fella's first book, but then a searing hot panic and intense sense of dread began to set in. How on earth could I sum up my better half, the father of my children (as far as we know) and my best friend in a mere page or two? I began to develop the same nervous, clammy feeling I had when Sister Illuminata, an imposing Fransican nun, barked out that all of us 6th graders were to explain "what Jesus meant to us" in a haiku. Impossible!

To truly translate the gentle kindness and supreme weirdness that is Ben Falcone is no small task.

Do I address his incessant fear of being poisoned by anyone and everyone, and, very often, yours truly? Do I mention that he moons me at least three times a day and yet, after 11 years of marriage and 18 years together in total, I still never see it coming? How do I salute the fact that he has upwards of 11 blood pressure cuffs squirreled away in his closet?

Ben is my Maria from The Sound of Music (God that's two nun references—sorry): "How do you hold a hypochondriacal, toxicophobial moonbeam in your hand?"

Ben's kindness and his humor are woven into the fabric of his stories. His take on the world, his family, our kids and his own remarkable parents cannot be separated from the man he is. Ben and his stories are the sum of so many wonderful and weird parts. His love for our girls is baked into every word he writes about them—the same love I see in his eyes every day when the girls are climbing all over him and essentially trying to destroy him.

The world is crazy and sometimes overwhelming, but Ben has always had the gift of seeing humor and love in the smallest of moments, and heroes in the most unlikely of characters (I mean, He married me).

So it's okay if things sometimes get stressful in our life together. I know I can always soothe him by softly whispering in his ear, "My love, I promise that I have not poisoned you today" as I gently present him with a shiny new blood pressure cuff.

—Melissa McCarthy

PREFACE

I AM SITTING AT my daughter's school concert. Vivian, my oldest, is just nine years old, and she and all the other kids are lined up singing their brains out in the small chapel that doubles as an auditorium in their school. My wife and I are struggling to actually see her sing because of the phalanx of eager parents in front of us, holding up their phones, recording each and every moment. Some of the parents have their devices fully over their heads to get the perfect angle—it is a sea of phones as far as the eye can see, and phones are all my eyes can see. Every time Melissa and I look for Vivian, we see approximately six thousand devices, but not our kid. I am doing what I normally do when something irritating is happening: I am pretending to be calm while my blood pressure rises sharply.

As I stare at all these phones and finally catch a glimpse of one-sixteenth of my daughter's head, I am struck by a series of thoughts. When did I become *this* guy? I'm a full-fledged dad, upset to the point of yelling at the fact that he can't see his daughter sing on the stage. When did I become a person who raged at a bunch of crazy helicopter parents who are so busy trying to video their kids that they never actually watch them? When did I get this old? When did I get this cranky? Wasn't I just eight years old and singing in my own school concert not so long ago? Wasn't my dad just the guy watching me with a dazed smile on his face, much like the dazed smile I have plastered on mine? Did he catch my eye and whisper, "Good job, buddy," just as I did to Viv, somehow through the sea of Steve Jobs's legacy? And I think to myself, "When did things get so weird?"

Because let's face it, being a dad is weird. As the father of two daughters in Los Angeles, I am constantly put into weird situations that make me wonder how the hell I got there. The other day, I walked in my door and my dog was wearing goggles and there were two strangers in surgical scrubs holding her.

My daughter Vivian calmly informed me, "Gladys is get-

ting a cold laser treatment. Don't worry, Dad. She *likes* it."
My dog did indeed seem to be enjoying the attention, so I
smiled and walked toward the kitchen to grab some grapes.
My own unique set of circumstances being a father is mostly
wonderful, sometimes maddening, and certainly weird. Was
it all this wonderful and weird for my own dad back in the
1970s and '80s, as he sat there fresh out of graduate school in
Southern Illinois, watching his child sing songs that celebrate
the seasons? What would my dad have done if he couldn't see
me sing because everyone had their stupid cell phones and
tablets in front of his face?

Of course in the 1980s there were no cell phones. But if
there had been phones and tablets at that time, and if people
were holding them in front of my dad's face at my concert,
I am quite certain that he would not have remained silent,

as I have. Instead, he would have said something subtle like, "Put those goddamn things away before I shove them up your ass."

As I stare for what seems like forever at that glowing wall of phones, thinking about my old man, I see the truth.

I AM A DAD. I'm not even a young dad. My daughters are nine and six, and I wasn't a teenager when they were born. And in many ways, I'm nothing like my old man. I would never tell people to stick their phone where the sun don't shine, or something equally cutting and frank, even though sometimes (let's be honest, often) I really want to.

But in some ways, I am a lot like my dad. I have carried a lot of my father into my journey as a parent. He definitely taught me some things, and many of his ideas rubbed off on me.

But how many? Has my somewhat unusual upbringing affected how I raise my daughters? And will I ever have the courage to tell people to shove their electronics, like my dad would have done? All of this requires some examination. Hence, this book.

First things first, let's start off by taking a look at my father. Here he is:

His name is Steve Falcone and he is a truly great guy. He is fearless, thunderously loud, ferociously funny, and has a propensity for wearing hats. This is a fairly recent photo of

him, and I think it sums him up pretty well. Please note that though he is wearing a track suit and a sparkly hat, which would imply that he would not take himself too seriously, he is also holding his glasses jauntily to the side and looking importantly into the camera, which implies that he is indeed someone serious—and not to be trifled with. This simple yet complex essence sums up my father. Yet in another way, it only scratches the surface.

I learned a lot from Steve Falcone—good things, bad things, weird things, and some in between. My dad is seventy-three now, and he's been a good father to me and an excellent grandfather to my daughters. He's taught me many things, among them that advice given sparingly is advice likely followed. (When I began to get bad grades in high school he pulled me aside and said, "Getting shitty grades is no way to get out of this little town, son." Boom! Good grades followed immediately.) He taught me to always say what's on your mind, which is advice I actually never took—my mind is a sea of unsaid thoughts sometimes pried loose with too much coffee or scotch. He taught me that being there for your child was the best thing of all—whether times were good, bad, ugly, or just plain weird.

This book is a collection of stories about the great, albeit strange adventure of fatherhood. Some of the stories are about my experiences as a dad, and some are about my experiences with my dad. There are recollections from my childhood in Southern Illinois and my life now in Los Angeles. I will try to capture the things I've learned from my dad and about being a dad through stories—many of which are embarrassing. Did my father used to semi-regularly fall asleep on the roof of our home? Of course he did, dear reader. Why? Because he had imbibed a few Jamesons and wanted to see the stars, of course. Have I personally ever peed in a closet? Yes. Of course. Why? Because I was so exhausted as the father of a newborn that I was convinced it was the bathroom. You see, I am willing to embarrass myself to help out my fellow dads, so they feel less alone in their own weirdnesses, as we all should. I'd also like to help mothers, because I am not sexist. I'm just not. So I truly hope that some of the parental advice found here will be useful to all the parents out there. But mostly, I hope that you, dearest reader and my new best friend, will laugh a few times as you read these pages. At the very least, know this: if you are the guy with the phone held high at the school concert, chances are there are parents around you who want to shove it up your ass.

Have Good Times

or The Value of Adult Friendships for the Sanity of Parents and Children Alike

MY DAD LIKES GOOD times. Good times are important to him. His idea of a good time is being over at a friend's house, laughing and drinking with all of his other friends. He likes to sit around, listening to his friends tell stories and telling stories of his own. If someone has a new story worth telling, all the better. If not, someone will tell an old one and get laughs like it was the first time they told it. That seems the perfect recipe for a good time with friends, if you ask me.

I grew up in this series of my parents' friends' houses, in the "Little Egypt" section of Southern Illinois (why they named it that, I do not know). These houses were full of laughter and booze. I remember my childhood as being at someone's house every weekend, sometimes on weeknights too, and being surrounded by loud and funny adults. For a quick review of the cast, we had Dan Seiters, who would write semi-erotic short stories and sign them "Rosemary Finnegan" because she was the only member of the group who thought the stories were a bit too lewd. Everyone laughed and told Dan to stop, as they simultaneously hoped to hell he never would. (He never will. My favorite story involves a female character who constantly is drawing rabbits on her boobs. I forget why. Maybe I'll ask Rosemary Finnegan.)

My parents met all of their friends while they were in graduate school in the English Department at Southern Illinois University. They met some of them at a great bar in Carbondale named The Pinch Penny Pub that was perfect for poor grad students. After a short, disastrous attempt at living in Texas, my parents put down roots in Carbondale, and most of their friends from grad school did the same. This group all led the simple yet fun lives of educated upper-middle-class people who lived in a liberal college town in a semirural conservative area of the state. In a land in which gun racks adorned the back of many a truck, these were the people who read *The New Yorker*, drove small Hondas, loved Greek food, and knew which bars had jazz bands on a Tuesday night.

They hung out together, partied together, saw movies together, and celebrated the birth of new kids in the group. When a family in the group had a new baby, they didn't disappear as parents today tend to; they simply kept going out with giant bags underneath their eyes and a tiny baby in tow. I admit that when the girls were first born, I "disappeared" for a while. Melissa and I didn't really see friends for a few months, but through grit, determination, and the desire to see the sky, we got back on track. But for my parents, there would be no hiding. The group was the social outlet that made the rest of life better. These people counted on each other for support, but mostly for fun.

My dad emerged as the de facto ringleader of this group and he revels in his role to this day. When he senses that the group needs to get together, he plans a party, which my mother then of course executes. When the party inevitably occurs, he will laugh loudly and often. If no one else has a joke, he'll laugh at his own.

One time I distinctly remember was when we were over at our friends Kelly and Cheri's house. Kelly, a big Chicagoan with a wonderful mustache (basically, he had the big, bushy king of all mustaches), worked for Budweiser and had a vending machine full of beer on his porch. It was a hot late-summer afternoon and we all sat on the porch as the adults drank beer and the kids drank soda. My father was wearing shorts but no underwear (he couldn't be bothered with underwear) and he was telling a very long story about growing up in Philadelphia. Cheri, a funny red-haired lady with a quick smile who married Kelly after they met working at The Pinch Penny, casually looked over at my dad and said, while he was mid-story, "Hey Steve, your ball's out." Dan Seiters, the wonderfully weird gray-haired writer whose greatest claim to fame was that he could "balance a fifty-pound owl on his cock" (I'm not sure how he came upon that discovery. Some things are better left unanswered), immediately broke into hysterical laughter. Dan Finnegan, Rosemary's husband, a quiet, kind, and dry man, said, "I just assumed that we were all supposed to have our balls out—I was concerned that I was late to the party." Everyone kept laughing and piling on. Dan Seiters's wife, Judy, a gray-haired, unassuming woman who is quite surely the sharpest person I've ever met, laughed so hard she snorted beer out of her nose.

My dad let them finish with a pious look on his face, and then quickly adjusted his shorts and resumed the story with not a word about the offending testicle. He wasn't one bit embarrassed, though he was perhaps a touch annoyed to have to restart his story at a crucial point. The mark of my father's

———

power is that though I'd make fun of him about that moment later, I let him continue through his story that night—because he was really enjoying himself, and he just couldn't (and he really *shouldn't*) be distracted by the fact that his testicle was out in the open for everyone on the porch to see. Perhaps at the time, he was a bit perturbed that his story got a few less laughs than his testicle did. But when his friends bring up the story today, which they still do, he's thrilled to be the center of a good story that gets a good laugh.

(My dad is definitely not wearing
underwear in this picture.)

That's my dad in a nutshell (KA-BOOM). And he helps keep the gang together. Even now, the group gets together twice a week to tell old stories, to laugh about their kids who are now spread all over this country like wonderful cream cheese, and to share pictures of their grandchildren on phones that they don't understand.

Here is a picture of some of my parents'
friends from way back. I am the barefoot kid.

My life today is very similar to that of my parents' back in the day. People may think that because I married a lovely lady who often makes movies, we live in some kind of ridiculous Hollywood *scene* where fabulous people are singing and dancing into the wee hours, and maybe there are trained acrobats and martial artists who also sing and dance, and nobody has even *heard* of mashed potatoes, but the reality is far different. We met most of our best friends at a comedy theater in Los Angeles called The Groundlings—I guess that was our version of grad school. It is a grad school for funny people, and my wife and I made friends there who we remain connected to because, well, they are loud and funny, just like my parents' friends. My idea of a perfect weekend is having all of our friends over for a barbecue. We'll tell jokes and drink scotch and eat good food, and all of our kids will tell us to let them play by themselves, because the adults are "too boring." We let them so we can drink more scotch and tell more jokes.

So I have followed in my father's footsteps. I firmly believe that hanging out with your family and friends is the key to happiness. And in this way, my father and I are the same.

The only difference is that I always wear underwear.

2

It's About Who You Know

or Why Having Feathered Friends Will Keep Your Kids from Worrying About Your Crappy Job

MY DAD DIDN'T REALLY have a steady job for a long time. He was the proud owner of a master's degree in English Literature that no one cared about, and so he stayed home with my brother Flynn and me while my mom worked long hours as a social worker. My dad kept himself busy writing novels, which had great titles and tons of wordplay. My favorite titles are *The Triple-Misted Mountain, The Tribula-tion of Benbo Jones*, and *The Drunken Truck*. They were works of fiction, and they haven't been published (yet). The rest of his time he spent enjoying his friends and looking for work. Once in a while he landed something, generally outside of his field, but it never lasted too long. Truth be told, he bounced around from job to job until I was about thirteen years old. He was a stay-at-home dad before being a stay-at-home dad was cool. Like most kids anywhere, anytime in the history of the universe, Flynn and I didn't question the fact that our dad stayed home with us when most dads didn't—we just rolled with it and hoped that he would make us a club sandwich. He was cheerful and fun to hang around with. He'd start blasting music early in the morning (he favored jazz and the soundtrack to the musical *Camelot*—I can recite every lyric to that musical to this day) and told the same jokes every morn-ing. Question: "How are you doing?" Answer (always): "Any better and I'd have to be twins." In short, even though things weren't "normal" for that time, we had a blast.

When I was very small, maybe in second grade, my dad got the best job yet. He worked for the Southern Illinois Uni-versity Arena, running the concession stands. Though this job paid just above minimum wage, the benefits were staggering to my brother and me. Dad would bring home cases of soda, giant packs of ice-cream sandwiches, and garbage bags full of popcorn. Flynn and I would wake up in the morning, see that giant bag and smell that sweet corn, and start screaming for my mom to open up the freezer. And then there they'd be: twenty, thirty ice-cream sandwiches, and the good cheap ones they sold at the arena. *Holy shit!* Show the seven-year-old me something better than a freezer full of vanilla-flavored corn syrup and chocolate-like cake. There was nothing better you could possibly ever show seven-year-old me. Unless you could take seven-year-old me into space, stand seven-year-old me on the moon with a bunch of cool astronauts, and then open up a freezer with thirty ice-cream sandwiches inside.

During my dad's tenure at this amazing job, "Sesame Street on Ice" came to the Arena, which in retrospect seems so typically '70s. All the characters skate around. Were they singing? What the hell were they singing? How much marijuana had these skating artists partaken of before they put on their Muppet costumes? I am not a scientist, but I guarantee 100 percent accuracy when I say the answer is a shitload. Of course I can't remember any of the show's actual content per se; all I can remember is that after the show, my dad took me on the ice, which was quite a thrill in and of itself, because not all kids got to do that. And that's when it happened. Big Bird was skating around, talking to some other kids (I didn't

———

have that kind of luck), and my dad said, "Hey Big Bird, can I introduce you to my son?" And then Big Bird just skated over to us casually, like this was not the biggest event in my life. My dad *fucking knew* Big Bird. This was a big deal. I stood there, shivering in terror and delight, with my eyes bugging out of my head. I could not speak. I would not speak. So Big Bird gave me a high-five. He said, "Nice to meet you." If I had grown up in the age of cell phones, I'd have a picture of the seven-year-old me with Big Bird. But in a very real way, I'm glad I don't have that picture. Something about the act of stopping the moment, taking a picture, and preserving this treasured time with Big Bird to flip through every so often on a cell phone would have cheapened it. Instead, I got a high-five. From an eight-foot-tall yellow bird who was pretty darn famous to the elementary school set. And nobody can take that away from me. And my dad made it happen. And my mom, too. She drove me to the show. Interestingly, I have no idea if my brother met Big Bird. He may have been too old for that kind of thing, or hanging with his friends up in the seats eating those amazing shitty ice-cream sandwiches—or maybe he wasn't there at all. My memory is focused on the yellow dude, and the fact that my dad was the guy who hooked me up.

This fine occasion is one of the big childhood moments that made my dad larger than life to me. To this day, he reminds me of this childhood event, which is another thing that makes him great. He takes the time to remind his forty-three-year-old son that he created a heavenly moment on the ice for him, many years ago—in a land of cheap, delicious ice-cream sandwiches and garbage-bag popcorn. In a land where there was so much soda in the fridge downstairs that my mom didn't know what to do, my brother and I did our best to help the crazy woman out. It was the least we could do, taking one for the team and all that. We suggested that if we each drank six sodas a day, we'd get through the stash in no time. Cooler heads may or may not have prevailed on that issue (Mom won. We were limited to one a day and however many we could sneak), and my dad kept bringing home the treats until he lost that job. I never really figured out why he was fired. I think it may have had something to do with the fact that he let everyone who worked for him bring home popcorn, ice-cream sandwiches, and soda. That was likely frowned upon by management.

Today I work several jobs at once. I enjoy my work and sometimes I have difficulty understanding the fact that I earn my living working as an actor, director, and writer. I had been doing these jobs for free for so long that Melissa and I both forget that we now get paid to do what we love. It's an incredible joy, one that I am so grateful for. This joy, of course, comes with a catch. The catch is guilt. For example, as I write this very book, for which I've been granted a reasonable amount of dollars to act as "author," I feel guilty that I am missing picking my kids up from school. See—no give without take. Because I enjoy writing and it's always been a dream to publish a book, I make the sacrifice of school pickup for a few days. I am a hard worker by nature, but if I didn't enjoy my jobs, I would surely not feel guilty about working at them. Yet because I enjoy working and I enjoy my children, I feel terribly guilty when work has to come before my dad duties. I don't think my dad felt guilt for working, but for different reasons. We were just trying to get by and he did what he could to help out. My mom made more money than he did back then (a situation mirrored in my own life) as he bounced around trying to get that master's degree to work for him. He was just holding up his end of the bargain. He missed a few bedtimes. The Big Bird thing may have made him feel good, too. I have a feeling it did, which is why he still brings it up.

When I was thirteen, my dad came into the house and told my brother and me that he had a "major announcement." He was wearing a corduroy jacket and he looked like the kind of guy who might smoke a pipe, probably something like this . . .

No big deal, but in this photo I seem to be
getting a pretty major fucking award.

He took my brother Flynn and me out to the front porch
and sat us down.

"Boys. I got a job." This announcement was highly irregu-
lar. He was constantly getting jobs, and they were very tempo-
rary. So what was the big deal? Why the big announcement
this time? My mom looked very happy, too, so I asked him
what kind of job it was.

"I'm going to teach English at John A. Logan Community College."

My brother took a long beat.

Then he yelled, "Holy shit, Dad got a real job! We're rich!"

My mom and I laughed and we all gave my dad a big hug. He was very excited. He went on to teach at that college for many, many years. That master's degree finally had a use— and the job at the college was one that my father very much enjoyed. And I don't believe he felt guilty about that, either. He'd tried a long time to make a good living doing something he loved, and I'm pretty sure he didn't waste his time feeling guilty when he achieved what he'd worked hard for.

So that is something that I'm trying to remember: working hard is not a crime. And isn't it a good thing for your kids to see you doing your best at something you love to do? It's something that I still struggle with, and I'm sure will always struggle with. My kids haven't met Big Bird, but they've traveled a lot and seen some really neat things. Yet I, like many parents in these modern times, constantly feel like I could be doing more—showing them better things, spending more time with them, making every day a spectacular adventure that blows everyone's mind.

Back when my dad had his job at the SIU Arena, I took a field trip with my second-grade class. We went to the student center at SIU, and thinking back now I wonder why they were taking a bunch of seven-year-olds to a college student center. To watch twenty-year-olds play arcade games while they slowly, imperceptibly flunked out of school? It doesn't matter, because what I do remember is seeing my thirty-eight-year-old dad walking down the hallway as I stood in line with my class. I screamed out, "Daddy!" and ran up to him. He grabbed me and lifted me into a big hug. Worlds had collided. I don't know what I thought my parents did when I went to school—I guess I figured they just disappeared until I came home, and then they reappeared like magic, hopefully with some kind of fun plan, ice-cream sandwiches, or the decision that we could stay up late. But there he was, in real life. It was sometime in the fall, the air was crisp, and my dad appeared out of thin air in a smoky student center and gave me a hug. Better than Big Bird.

———

3

Take It All in Stride

or Nothing Is Too Big of a Deal

LOOK AT THIS GUY. Does he seem worried to you? Exactly. From the plastic booze cup in his hand (I'm pretty sure it's full of an inexpensive chardonnay), to his silly orange lei, to the charming foam sombrero on his head, everything in this

picture says, "Hey, we're here to have a good time." Add my dad's getup to the fact that he is looking at the picture taker (a picture I am sure *he* requested in the first place) with a look like, "What are you looking at?" and you have quite simply the epitome of a carefree man. Not a worry in the world for this guy.

Hmmm . . . NOT worrying too much. That's a novel concept for parents in today's world, myself very much included. It seems like I went from a kid who never worried (or at least not that much, and if I did, it was probably about things like "Are the leaves in this cardboard box scratchy?").

To a young man who worried just a bit more about slightly bigger things. Grades. Money (or lack thereof). Getting laid (or lack thereof).

To a forty-year-old who was instantly convinced that the sky was falling flat on my head.

I am aware that I am not forty years old in this picture, but does this child not look like he will grow into someone who fears a head injury?

Which led me to a very real fear of concussions. (Along with the fact that I once got a mild concussion while filming a *fucking sitcom*—really? Sad but true: I was supposed to be hit in the head with a rubber stapler, and yes it was only a rubber stapler, but the person I was acting with hit me in the head with that sucker real hard! Then I was told to improvise a bunch, as no one knew that I was concussed. I simply do not need help getting worse at improvising, gang.) So now among all of my other fears and concerns, I have a very real belief that I can get a concussion from combing my hair too hard. So I take it slow and easy with this gorgeous mane of mine.

All of that pales in comparison to the worrying I do about my kids. I worry—oh how I worry—about my kids. Is all of this worry a product of today's world being so connected through the Internet and social media, which I barely understand? Do worries compound and grow exponentially, like some kind of math calculation that I also barely understand?

Let's compare my very real fear of concussions to my dad's attitude toward anything medical. Several years ago, my dad had surgery to remove a mole on his back. This wasn't one of those slice-it-off-quick, Band-Aid, in-and-out sort of things. This was a deep drilling, where they get rid of the mole and the area around it, then send it all to the lab to be analyzed. And guess what? My dad didn't even tell me. If I were going through that kind of procedure, trust me—everyone in my path would have known. Friends, family, strangers. Why? Because I would keep them fucking updated. Because that stuff is scary and by sharing it, it's less scary. My dad didn't even bother to tell me. And neither did my mom. Why? Because they didn't want me to worry? Nope. They didn't tell me because it was no big deal to them. If something had become a big deal, they would have let me know. But it wasn't, so nobody even mentioned it at all—UNTIL A YEAR LATER!

Thing is, they're right on this one. And I'm wrong. There's no need to sweat all the small stuff. When my older daughter was two years old, she poked herself in the eye while running with a stick (yes, I was telling her not to do that, but she was so damn *fast*) and it got all red and weird and she was crying at 5 p.m. on a Friday—of course, right when the doctor's office was closing. As we raced there, I spoke with a soothing voice to her as my blood pressure skyrocketed. I imagined every worst-case scenario possible, including the idea that as we received heartbreaking news about the eye from the doctor, Los Angeles would be hit by a devastating nuclear strike in an ironic double whammy. Anyway, her eye turned out to be just fine and my panic was unwarranted. I make an effort to be less fragile around my kids, and to instill in them a healthy "this is not a big deal" attitude when they do something like skin their knees, and my acting challenge is to not panic when they get an injury. I have also told my kids that chocolate cures wounds. I am sort of scared that they're going to start hurting themselves on purpose just to get a piece of chocolate, but it's the cost of doing business.

Lately, in an effort to emulate my father a bit more, I have been making some efforts to take things less seriously. And I think that I am making some real progress. Here's some evidence:

Doesn't this guy look like he doesn't sweat the small stuff?

4

The Big Sky Theory

or Sometimes It's Okay to Lie to Your Kids

I WAS PROBABLY FOURTEEN years old when I realized that my dad is full of shit. We were taking a road

---

trip together in his red Honda CR-X. Look at this sweet beast:

It was the '90s, and I thought this car was the very definition of cool. It had no backseat, which never stopped my dad, brother, and me from using it for long road trips. I would usually straddle the non-backseat and say over and over again, "It's not that bad. Pretty comfortable," while my nether regions became more and more tender with each mile. It was a small price to pay to ride in a chick magnet such as this.

My dad had a history of buying pretty shitty cars, and once he was secured in his job as an English teacher at John A. Logan College, he went ahead and splurged on this, the most awesome of all sports cars in the history of sports cars. The Honda CR-X and Mazda Miata will forever battle for the sacred place on top of the mountain of snazzy sports vehicles. He made his choice, and the CR-X was ours!

Once my brother left home for college at the University of Chicago, my dad and I would take this cherry-red CR-X all over the country. We had many adventures while I was in high school, like the time we went to Greeley, Colorado, to hang out with an acquaintance whom my father referred to as "Dr. Bong." Dr. Bong was teaching some classes at Colorado State University, and he lived in a small apartment filled with coffee and weed. He spoke fondly of the "synergy" that he felt when he had lots of good coffee and weed. He never seemed all that stoned to me, and I have no idea what course he taught. I probably smoked some of his weed, which I don't recall, but I remember I was not fond of his coffee.

My mom was curiously absent from these adventures, which usually involved sleeping on someone's couch and long drives through the night. The strange thing is, my mom can drive longer and farther than any other human on this earth. All she needs is the most coffee that any human can drink and good weather, and she can actually drive forever. So in retrospect, it must not have been the length of the trip, but rather the quality of the accommodations that kept her saying "maybe next time" when we invited her. I would have given her the passenger's seat. But, my mom is smart.

The trip when I discovered my father was full of shit was when we decided to drive from Carbondale, Illinois, to Key West, Florida. One of my father's many passions is Hemingway. And Key West is where Hemingway had spent some time. So off we went.

———

My dad and I had some great long talks on the road, as you may imagine. He is a great conversationalist, far better than me. In fact, he barely needs another person to respond. He can just keep talking. His conversations/monologues are somewhat legendary for their length and entertainment value. On one road trip, we wrote a book of dirty limericks together that seem just as good or bad as every other book of dirty limericks that has or has not been written. One I can remember off the top of my head:

There was a young man from Dubuque
His gas could make you puke
He could clear a room when he started to boom
That's why his nickname was Nuke.

As I reread this, it's a pretty bad limerick. Truth be told, are there any good limericks? And in our defense, I don't think we laughed as loud at that one as at some of the others. But that's the one that remains etched in my mind. I haven't told it to the girls. I'm too afraid that they'll think it was funny.

On our drives, my dad would tell me fascinating stories about growing up Italian in hardscrabble Philadelphia, in a Catholic family with a million brothers and lots of pasta. This is good stuff, the things they make movies about. There's one story in particular that really blows my mind. My father is one of five brothers. He was close with all of them, but his brother Nick was my dad's best friend. He was the best man at my mom and dad's wedding, and they were as close as they can be. And then one day, Nick just took off. Poof! No one had any clue where he was, though the family seemed pretty sure Nick was alive and living somewhere in Nevada. My Uncle Gene (a fireman and Vietnam veteran) hired a private detective to find him, and though I don't know the details, he learned that Nick was alive and out West somewhere. But for whatever reason, my dad and his brothers made no attempt to find him. Of course, I have my theories—witness protection, living under a new identity as a fugitive from the law. But that is pretty wild stuff—I mean, how many people do you know whose brother *dis-a-fucking-ppeared*? My dad's did. Uncle Nick, if you're reading this, I have to say—weird move, man. Weird. Here's another thing: my dad gets curiously quiet when discussing my uncle's disappearing act—it's the one subject he doesn't love to discuss. Once in a while he'll opine as to why he disappeared and say, "Maybe he was a second-story man." And I'll say, "What, like a burglar?" And my dad will sort of look into the distance and pretend that he didn't hear the question.

This is a picture of my uncles Gene, Nick, Mike, and Kevin.
(I have obscured Uncle Nick's face just in case he's on the
lam.) My dad is the one in the kick-ass white pants.

So back to the CR-X. My dad and I were in the CR-X on the way to Key West and having a discussion, presumably my dad was doing most of the talking (definitely not about my Uncle Nick), the sun was setting somewhere off the Florida highway, and it was just beautiful. There weren't many other cars on the road and I kept looking out at the gorgeous pink light. Our conversation went like this:

ME:

Wow, it's so pretty out. The sky looks
bigger here.

———

MY DAD:

It is. It's bigger here.

ME:

Huh. Wow. (*now skeptically*) Really?

MY DAD:

Yeah. The science of it is strange, but
yeah, the sky is a lot bigger here than it
is in Illinois.

ME:

Wow.

MY DAD:

Crazy, I know. But that's because it is
closer to the equator.

ME:

But isn't the horizon line, like, flat?

MY DAD:

Well, yeah. But as you get farther
south . . .

ME:

The horizon gets lower or something?

———

MY DAD:

That's right. The horizon gets lower as you go farther south. That's how it is.

ME:

Dad.

MY DAD:

What?

ME:

Did you hear about this somewhere?

MY DAD:

What, "The Big Sky Theory"?

ME:

Yeah. Did you read it, or learn it somewhere?

MY DAD:

No. I think I might have made it up.

I started to laugh pretty hard at that. Not because my dad had lied to sound smart, because that would be less funny to me. What I am sure happened is that my dad truly believed "The Big Sky Theory" as he said it, and was certain that it *was* true as the words came out of his mouth. And only by my questioning him about it did he even realize that he had made it up. I think that a lot more people do this than we think. I think people say something and the minute it pops out of their mouth, they believe it to be true. I am pretty sure that I do it daily or at least weekly with my daughters.

In fact, here are a few of the things I have told my daughters that I believed to be true upon saying them, and upon further reflection I have come to doubt their factual integrity. I have told my daughter these "lies" in moments when they needed answers and I needed to provide them. None of this was done maliciously in any way, of course. It was only after the fact that I realized that perhaps I may have given them a wonderful ration of crap.

- Everyone they've ever known who died is in heaven. (Note: Melissa's mom, Sandy, talks about heaven in a way that makes it sound like a nice suburb. When my mother-in-law does something thoughtful for someone, for example, makes sure that everyone in the house who would possibly want coffee has coffee in front of them, she will say things like, "You're getting another shingle on your house in heaven." Which leads me to think, "Who's putting on the shingle? Are there workers in heaven? Or do you know how to do roof work automatically when you go to heaven?

———

Or does God just put on a new shingle when it rains? Does it rain in heaven?" Every time you start to try to describe what heaven looks or feels like, the conversation begins to feel dicey. Also, I personally believe in heaven but I leave the details vague, even for myself.)

• Reincarnation is real.

• Bugs have feelings.

• The alternator is an important part of a car.

• Bugs are capable of feeling the feeling of love. Like, they love other bugs and their bug mommies and bug daddies and sisters and brothers.

• There are an infinite number of galaxies; therefore there must be aliens. (Actually, this seems completely reasonable to me.)

• Everything I've ever told them regarding math.

Back in the CR-X, my dad started laughing pretty hard too, realizing that he had unintentionally lied to me with his horseshit "Big Sky Theory." I thought for a moment and then said . . .

ME:

How full of shit are you?

MY DAD:

I'm pretty full of shit, son.

ME:

What other stuff have you told me that you made up?

(A beat).

MY DAD:

All of it?

We laughed so hard that we had to pull the car over and finish watching the sunset underneath that big Florida sky. That huge, enormous, false Floridian sky.

—

5

Rip Off the Band-Aid

or The Argument for Truth Once in a While

I **WAS IN THE FOURTH GRADE.** At my school, when the day was over, we would wait in line for our buses in the gymnasium. When the buses were ready for us, we'd walk outside in a very chaotic fashion, step inside the correct bus, and find our seats. Of course the bus line was a time for lots of conversation among the kids, and since all the grades were jumbled up, it was a real free-for-all of young society.

It was one day in that bus line that I was told there was no Santa Claus. I can't remember the face of the older kid who told me, and I think I've replaced him in my mind with Scut Farkus, the bully with braces from the movie A *Christmas Story*. That character was a real asshole to Ralphie. And so was the kid who did this to me. I mean, what kind of asshole feels the need to tell an eight-year-old that there's no Santa Claus? If everyone would just stop telling everyone else there's no Santa Claus, then we'd all just grow up believing in Santa Claus from our first Christmas to our last. What's wrong with that? Maybe I'm just a jolly old elf, but jeez, what's the harm in letting kids just believe?

STOP TELLING PEOPLE THERE'S NO SANTA CLAUS.

THANK YOU.

So I went home crying. I cried on the bus, I cried on the walk home, and I cried when I got to my house. And I sat in our little den, crying. Because I was thinking everything over, and wondering if maybe this asshole kid was right. Maybe there *was* no Santa. And I saw my dad, darting back and forth past the doorway, and I knew he was trying to figure out how best to play this situation and also to figure out why in the hell his eight-year-old son was crying like a baby.

I started getting nervous, because I heard my brother whisper, "Some kid said there was no Santa Claus," to which my dad replied, "Ah, shit." I heard my dad pacing back and forth, asking my brother where my mother was. This was serious. My dad knew my mother was at work. She was always at work, doing her job as a social worker securing grant money for worthy programs. It was just my dad at home, as he usually was when I was that age. If he was upset enough that he forgot that my mom was at work, this was a serious situation. Maybe that asshole kid was telling me the truth. This was turning into the worst day of my life.

Dad paced around for maybe half an hour, and I stopped crying. I was no longer thinking about that kid and the possibility of life without Santa Claus; I was thinking, "What the fuck is wrong with my dad?"

Finally, when I couldn't possibly cry another second, or listen to my dad pace around like a crazy person anymore, I called my father over to me. I was lying on the couch, exhausted.

He shuffled through the door and over to me. "So a kid said there's no Santa, huh?"

"Yeah."

"Jesus Christ. Who does that?"

And I said the asshole kid's name. And then, I went for it. I had to. I had to know.

"Is it true?"

He sighed and said, "Yeah, buddy. I'm sorry. It's true."

And I started to cry all over again. My dad rubbed my back and told me it was okay to cry, and that Santa was a good thing to believe in, he was the spirit of Christmas and that was an important idea. I could be making this part up, but I believe he started paraphrasing, "Yes, Virginia, there is a Santa Claus." My dad made me feel better, eventually. I knew I was probably too old to believe in Santa anyway, but I just did because I really wanted to. And because nobody had ever told me that he wasn't real, until that day.

"You gonna be okay, buddy?" my dad asked as he got up from the couch after our big moment, after this excellent display of parenting.

"I think so."

And he paused a second, mulling something over in his head. I could tell there was something else he wanted to say.

"What, Dad?"

"You might as well know, there's no Tooth Fairy or Easter Bunny, either."

And my brother, who'd been out of sight up until this point, listening with his ear against the den door, yelled out, "Holy shit, Dad!"

"What? He was gonna find out soon enough! These are the more minor characters anyway!"

I stared at my dad in horror and screamed, *"What the fuck are you doing?"*

He ignored the swear word and shrugged. "I had to do it—it's like ripping off a Band-Aid!"

My brother staggered into the room at this point, laughing his ass off. Then, he came over and gave me a hug.

"You okay?"

"Yeah, I'm okay, but what's so funny?"

Flynn looked over at my dad and started laughing again. "You really went for it, Dad! Good grief."

My dad looked at my brother and simply said, "You gotta go for it, son. I stand by my decision."

And that's how in the space of twenty seconds, I learned that Santa and the minor characters were all fakes—but that in the bigger scheme of things, everything was okay.

I hope that my daughters never meet that asshole kid who will tell them that Santa isn't real, but if they do, I might combine everything just like my pop did and get the truth all out there in one fell swoop. I don't know. My older daughter just loves the Easter Bunny. So she'd disagree that he's a minor character. And my younger daughter is still in first grade. With any luck, she won't meet that asshole kid for another couple of years.

———

Here's Scut Farkus, from *A Christmas Story*.
Yes, that's the correct spelling. (Shown here
with his other bully buddy, Grover Dill.)

Note: As I have been working on this book, time is of course passing. Vivian, my older daughter, is definitely catching on to the whole Santa thing. And I blame the parents at her school for this. It's because of St. Patrick's Day. The kindergarten kids all made a "leprechaun trap," which is a cute thing, right? Sure it is! It's a cereal box that they decorate and then put a hole in, so the leprechaun will get "trapped." Cool, right? Except that the parents at my school filled their kids' goddamn traps with candy. I had NO IDEA that this would be happening, because, who knew? The lies have all gone too far. We now leave carrots for the reindeer and put out fake snow on Christmas Eve, and kids are treated to more and more wonder, and they're going to feel that rug pulled out from under them all that much harder when their Scut

Farkus tells them the truth. So, the other parents filled the traps with candy and the kids came to school the day after St. Patrick's Day proudly showing off the loot that their leprechauns left them. And Georgie was really sad because she didn't catch any candy. Or a leprechaun. So I did what any dad would do: I lied to her and told her that leprechauns are notoriously fickle folks and sometimes they come the day after St. Patrick's Day. And I put candy in the goddamn leprechaun trap. And my lovely daughter Vivian, who is not stupid, came up to me that morning and said, "Dad, did *you* put the candy in the leprechaun trap?" I was quite sure that my eyes darted left and right in a classic and probably exaggerated version of what a liar looks like, and I said, "No, honey. Leprechaun." And I quickly walked away, sweating like a beast.

Leprechaun traps? Now we have to commit to magic on St. Patrick's Day? What's next? The enchanted ghost of Christopher Columbus, who leaves good little girls and boys pans of lasagna?

And said with massive amounts of respect and love, to whoever created "Elf on the Shelf" . . . Fuck you. Fuck you, you fucking monster.

———

6

Parenting Through Hypochondria

or The Time I Thought I Might be Gay

I WAS A BIT of a hypochondriac growing up. I got a hernia when I was in first grade and another one in eighth grade, and had to have surgery for each. They were successful surgeries, but to this day I still do not like going to the doctor. I have the fear that against my will, I will be placed in the hospital and everyone there will see what is really, really wrong with me. Which, I fear, is everything.

So as a kid, I didn't enjoy going to sleep, as I was consistently afraid that I would not wake up. If I got a stomachache, I was sure that there was something deeply wrong with me. Also, my brother had a stinging feeling when he peed one time and the doctors elected to put a tube in his urethra to figure out what was wrong, which was nothing. The only problem with the treatment of my brother's nonexistent problem is that when they placed the fucking tube *in his urethra*, he experienced what he still describes as the most pain he's ever had in his life. When I imagine that terrible moment in the doctor's office for my dear brother, I believe he was probably around this age:

At least he was rocking some sweet sweaters when he had to go through that terrible ordeal. I am sorry, Flynn. I should not add the cheap shot of showing you in this sweater to the incredibly painful urethra story. But I am, as you know, immature.

So anyway, I had a real fear of doctors, needles, stomach problems, headaches. You name it, I had it. And sometime during the ninth grade, my hypochondria amped up to a bizarre new level. I developed a case of what I can only describe as "homosexual panic." Now, before you start calling me a homophobe because by connecting hypochondria and homosexuality I must be insinuating that being gay is an illness, that's not what I mean at all. That's the opposite of my intention. Being gay is clearly just how you're born, gang. And it's great. And people who don't like gay people simply because they're gay are 100 percent people you don't want to hang out with. Also, not to go on a rant, but who cares who other people are attracted to or who they date or marry, or how they live their lives? Big dumb dummies, that's who. But I digress.

Anyway, here's what was really going on with me: I wasn't so much afraid that I would wake up one day and prefer guys to ladies. I was more afraid that I would wake up one day with some sort of amnesia, and not know who I was. And as a by-product, the new person that I became might be gay. I was also afraid that I didn't really know myself at all, and that my deep lack of identity and self-knowledge meant that perhaps I was gay and didn't know it. It wasn't about being upset about being gay. It was about being afraid of not knowing who I was. Like I said, I was kind of a worrisome child.

The other thing is that back then, being gay was much more mysterious than it is now. It wasn't something so out in the open, on television or in movies. That's not a good thing, but it is the truth. There was a guy in my high school named Waylon Jennings who was probably gay. (His name has been changed in case he is not out yet, or never was gay in the first place. Also, I love Waylon Jennings.) We all knew he probably was, though he never said so. To my knowledge, he was never bullied; the "cooler types" in our class just gently ostracized him. He wound up active in the Yearbook Club, along with a beautiful girl I was too afraid to ask out because she was African-American. I thought she was the smartest and nicest girl in class and I was certainly attracted to her (which did not inhibit my homosexual panic in the least), but I was afraid that the other kids would not accept us, as there were no interracial couples in my school. And I figured she probably didn't like me, anyway. I was a picture of courage and confusion.

So with all of this fear and madness running around in

my brain, I went home one night and told my father I was
worried that I would wake up one day and be gay.

My dad, being the guy he is, just smiled.

"Well, do you prefer guys or girls?"

"Girls."

"I don't really think that changes."

"But what if it does?"

"Then you'd be gay, and you'd be fine."

And with that, hypochondria cured. At least for that round
of "symptoms."

Then he looked at me and said, "Wanna shoot some
hoops?"

And we went and shot hoops.

Kids have their fears and their worries, just like we parents
do. So far neither of my girls has exhibited my hypochondriac
tendencies, thank the bard. In fact they both take things easy
on me, as I'm the fragile one in the family. When they bump
their heads they immediately say, "It wasn't hard, Dad. I'm
fine." My kids know that I battle hypochondria and they know
that I am certainly winning. That doesn't change the simple
fact that we are all going to die from the hantavirus, and there
isn't much we as parents can do about it. Except constantly
wash our hands and treat bottles of hand sanitizer as the life-
saving devices that they truly are.

One thing I can proudly say is that whether I am a hypo-chondriac or not (I am), my kids have thus far come to me with all of their problems and concerns in the world, just like I came to my dad. And I like to believe that I listen fully to them, and give them loving and rational advice, or sometimes just a hug after they've said their piece. That line of commu-nication between my children and myself is something I'll cherish and celebrate. I would celebrate that fact more openly and loudly if we weren't all going to die from the hantavirus in less than two years. That fucking hantavirus really helps you keep your head on straight.

7

Not All Vacations with Your Children Are Magical

or Never Take Travel Advice from a Bird-watcher

DURING THEIR FRESHMAN YEAR of high school, my brother's best friend, Stephen Merritt, moved from Carbondale to Columbia, South Carolina. Flynn and Steve managed to remain friends despite the distance, and during summer vacations, Dad, Flynn, and I would pile into the aforementioned

---

CR-X and drive to visit Steve. During these trips, Flynn and Steve would go off to do the two things that high school boys do most—sneak around to try to find booze, and chase girls. These two had a great time, laughing and goofing off. They would include me as much as they could in their plans, but as I was three years younger, there were severe limitations to what I could participate in. And, after a while, the older dudes wanted their space. It was understandable. This was a period in our lives when my brother and I looked more or less like this:

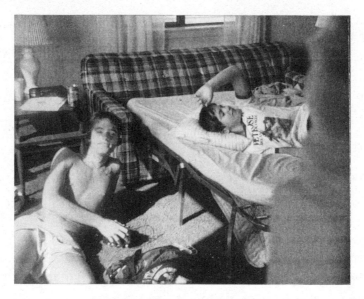

(Whoa, Flynner! Nice nips!)

So anyway, one year, my dad and I dropped my brother off to meet Steve and some of Steve's new friends in Myrtle

Beach, South Carolina. We left them in a cheap and dumpy hotel that reeked of old, cheap beer, where everyone in the place was probably quoting *Risky Business* and yelling about how awesome Porsches were. It was the 1980s after all. To my fifteen-year-old eyes, this hotel looked like heaven on earth. It was Spring Break and there were pretty girls in bathing suits walking up and down the streets. And then someone told me that Vanna White, from *Wheel of Fortune*, was originally from Myrtle Beach. My mind was literally *blown*. If you are not familiar with Myrtle Beach, it is a resort town on the South Carolina coast known for its golf courses, family vacations, and having a bitchin' Spring Break. If you are not familiar with the concept of Spring Break in Myrtle Beach, it is the week when college kids from Southeastern schools flock to the beach before the tourist season officially begins, and pretend it is warm enough to walk around in bathing suits constantly, drink their faces off, and do nothing but try to get laid. The locals are all scandalized but all too happy to collect the money these dumb kids bring in. As long as they leave as fast as possible when the week ends.

When we got to the hotel room where we were going to leave Flynn, AC/DC was blasting. Steve's friends were all drinking beer, and holy shit, they were actually talking about how awesome Porsches were. Somebody actually quoted the line, "Porsche. There is no substitute." from *Risky Business*! I couldn't believe it. It was too perfect! My brother was being presented with the promise of fun, sun, and pretty ladies. Then Dad handed him a hundred-dollar bill and said, "Don't drive. Be careful. Have fun."

"Thanks, Pop," Flynn said, closing the door on my dad and me, leaving us in the crisp spring wind of South Carolina. Staring at that grimy hotel door and with the sound of half-drunk eighteen-year-old guys' voices sailing on the breeze, I felt . . . very jealous. How the hell did my brother get to stay in that gorgeous moldy room and get loaded while I hit the road with Pop going God knows where?

"So, where are we going again?" I asked.

"Ocracoke," he answered. "It's an island. Just off the coast of North Carolina. It is part of the Outer Banks."

"And who told you about this place?"

"Barb Randolph's boyfriend, Farley."

Barb Randolph is a wonderful lady, and one of the crowd that my parents run around with. She was dating a guy named Farley, whom I had not managed to meet at this point in my life. After this vacation I made it a point to never meet him.

"Oh," I said, not convinced by this man named Farley or his advice.

My dad, sensing my unease, figured he'd better come up with something to make this trip sound more appealing.

"He's a bird-watcher."

"Who's a bird-watcher?"

"Farley. The guy who told me about this island."

"So we're going to a place that we've never been, because a bird-watcher said it's good?"

"Yeah! Should be fun." I could tell my dad was trying to convince himself, too.

My dad and I drove down to the ferry and put the sweet red Honda CR-X on the boat. It was cold on the water. Spring seemed to be more robust inland, but the ride was nice enough, until it started to get really foggy. And even colder.

After about forty-five minutes heading straight out into the ocean, I asked my dad how far we had to go. He pulled out some sort of itinerary map or schedule.

"Oh, shit. This place is a little farther than I thought."

"How far?"

"Two and a half hours."

"OH MY FUCKING GOD."

Yeah. We were a swearing family. What's the big fucking deal?

"It's not a big deal, buddy."

"WE'RE GONNA DIE AT SEA."

This was a pretty big barge we were on, and I suddenly realized that there were only four cars or so on the whole thing. Because almost NO ONE was going to Ocracoke except for the red-faced captain, who definitely drank vodka

---

for breakfast and who was definitely not focused on driving the goddamn barge.

My dad said, "Jeez. Relax. It's going to be fun. "

But I could see in his eyes that my dad was worried, and he was also probably annoyed that I was being such a whiny little dick. I don't think I was a dick super often, but because I loved my dad so much, I was very sensitive to when he thought I was being a dick. I didn't like making my dad mad, so I tried to focus on my breathing as I watched the fog from the shitty death barge we were trapped on.

We did make it to Ocracoke alive, in what felt like seventy-two hours later. The island was small, quiet, cold, and foggy (come on, Farley, what the fuck?) and so much worse than Myrtle Beach that I couldn't believe my eyes. There were no girls in bathing suits. No beer-drinking teenagers. No cheap motels reeking of cheap beer and broken dreams.

My dad had the address for the house we had for the week, but no instructions to get us there. This was, mind you, before GPS and cell phones, but I wasn't all that worried, since from what I could tell the island was the size of the gym at the high school back in Carbondale. But to be safe, my dad used the pay phone at the ferry station to call the realtor he had rented the house from to ask for directions.

She answered the phone and bizarrely told him to go "halfway 'round the island, hug the water."

Dad had a hard time understanding her because of her swampy accent, and he made her repeat these insane directions several times. We hugged the water and went halfway 'round the island. Six hours later we found the house. It was small, boring, and dirty, with a green rug that smelled like a lot of cats had peed on it.

The rest of the trip went in a slow, torturous blur. The natural beaches that Ocracoke is known for refer not to the sandy shores filled with bikini-clad girls that we'd left behind. Natural beaches are mostly rocks. The wind whipped us mercilessly and got sand in my boom box. (The boom box was a joint present for my brother and me to celebrate my birthday and his graduation. And I had bitched and moaned that I had to share the present until my brother took me aside and whispered fiercely, "This is an expensive thing—they couldn't afford two of them. Don't be a *fuckface*." A belated thank-you for the reality check, Flynn.) The average age of the tourists was eighty-six. Because it was an island created for fucking bird-watchers. (Fucking Farley. *Come on, man.*) I needed an island for uninhibited girls determined to make a man out of husky shy Italian kids. But I got a rainy island full of old bird-watchers. We watched a lot of David Letterman.

To be fair, it wasn't like my dad had all that much fun. There were no bars or good restaurants, so there was nothing for him to do, either. One night the power went out at 8:30, presumably because of some sort of tropical monsoon. My dad and I went outside to see if the power had gone out for the whole neighborhood. No one was up and around, checking it out. The whole neighborhood was quiet and desolate. *Because everyone in the neighborhood was already asleep at 8:30 p.m.* And why shouldn't they be? This place was boring as hell.

The only bright spot of the entire week was getting to watch my dad attempt to ride a bike. My father is good at many things, but cycling is not one of them. Apparently, growing up in the 1950s in a scrappy part of Philly is not conducive for learning how to ride a bike in a super-mellow fashion. He kept falling off the bicycle, becoming more and more enraged, not at himself for his lack of skill but at the actual bike. After a particularly bad fall, he started yelling, "Stupid fucking bike. Stupid island! Fuck you, Ocracoke!" Or I might be making that part up. But it's fun to think he was yelling, "Fuck you, Ocracoke!" Because no offense, Ocracoke—you might be great for some people, but for fifteen-year-old Ben, you were a real shit-show.

My dad has since sincerely apologized for that trip to Ocracoke, saying more than once, "Why did I take advice from a bird-watcher? I should have thought a little harder about that one, buddy. I just figured we'd have a good time anywhere." I forgive him, of course. I mean, at least he can admit that taking advice from a bird-watcher, when you are not a bird-watcher, is not a good policy when it comes to your vacation plans. But how was my dad to know how lame Farley's taste in vacations was? He didn't have the Internet at his fingertips to google "Best spots to take a wimpy fifteen-year-old on the North Carolina shore."

But here's the thing. Of all the trips I took with my pop, that horrible trip to Ocracoke is one of my all-time favorites. How can you know the good ones unless you have a horrible one to measure them against?

I will never take the girls to Ocracoke—first of all Melissa wouldn't let me, and secondly I really don't care to relive that. But, I have been guilty of cooking up plans that I haven't thought through enough. After Melissa and I finished making *Tammy*, I decided that we should take a trip across country with the family to celebrate finishing our first movie together. Normally I let Melissa handle planning these things because I have a tendency to not think things through carefully enough, but I love road trips and I was not to be stopped. So I rented a huge RV and got us a nice driver to drive it and decided that Melissa and I, both exhausted from working eighty-hour weeks, would enjoy a six-day trip across country from upstate New York all the way to California, with our five-year-old and our two-year-old in tow. So we finished shooting our last scene of the movie at Niagara

Falls, and the next evening after shooting some press photos, decided we would have the driver drive through the night while we slept in the RV. I thought the girls would love looking at the country through the window as we rolled effortlessly toward home.

Eight minutes into the trip, Georgie, who was two years old at the time, put both hands in the air and yelled at the top of her lungs, "I have to get off this bus! I'm going *crazy!*" At that moment I knew we were in for a long disaster of a trip. Lots of car sickness. Not as many stops along the way as you'd think. Very difficult to sleep on a giant bus. The children didn't seem to want to watch me look out the window and sip coffee and make pithy comments about the size of our beautiful country. One very disappointing Old West town tourist trap. Lots and lots of Nebraska. We finally got through the endlessness that is Wyoming and made it to Lake Tahoe, where I promptly got altitude sickness. Perhaps that trip was my children's Ocracoke. However, they were both too young to remember it forever, so I'm pretty sure I got away with it. But their version of Ocracoke looms before them, as sure as the sun will rise tomorrow. I will take my children on an awful vacation that they remember always. I really do want to see the Redwoods, and that trip has a pretty good chance of being a disaster.

A Quick Review:

This is Myrtle Beach.

This is Ocracoke.

8

Navigating Breakfast Conversations

or My Dad Never Had to Deal with This Stuff

I OFTEN HAVE BREAKFAST with my two girls. My little one is a bit of a wild card. She has a lot of energy and doesn't take shit from anybody. She's curious, too, and she's been asking me about what happens when you die. I quickly change the subject and usually challenge her to a race. Once while staying at a hotel, as the hotel maid was cleaning our room, my younger kid explained to me that "We're all going to die." She continued, "You're gonna die, Mommy's gonna die," and then she pointed at the maid. "I mean, look at her. That lady's going to die." I shushed her about seven seconds too late, and the maid looked back at me, concerned. I apologized. Then my little girl looked at me, all confidence, and said, "Daddy, God's going to kill me, too. *But I'm coming back.*"

My older daughter was born a devout Christian. Sometimes she looks out her open window, holding a cross. No shit. She stares at the sky, holding her small golden cross. I have to assume she's praying.

So this one morning, my kids were eating their gluten-free pancakes (KA-FUCKING-BOOM! I am a great dad!) and my then-three-year-old looked up at her mom and said, "Boy, God sure did give me an itchy vagina." My wife looked away, trying not to laugh as I instantly panicked.

But my daughter continued. "I mean, man. It's really itchy." I began to focus on astrally projecting myself to anywhere but where I was at that moment. I mean, if I tried hard enough, it would work, right?

The tiny blond child took a pause. I praised all that was holy that she was done. But oh no. There was more.

"Whoooo. It's just super itchy. So God made me have an itchy vagina."

My older child, being fully pious, gets very offended by

this kind of chatter. She was compelled by the spirit to correct her sister, posthaste.

"Georgie! God would never give you an itchy vagina. He might kill you, or strike you blind, but he would never give you an itchy vagina." My wife, no longer able to keep it in, burst out laughing, as my older daughter demanded to know what was so funny. I began to clear the plates from the table (people may have still been eating but I didn't care). I just had to get those plates to the sink; that way I could put another four feet of distance between myself and this "situation."

I realized that I was doing exactly what my dad, and maybe all dads, would do in such a delicate situation.

Not that my dad ever had to hear anything like this at the breakfast table, BECAUSE HE HAD BOYS, but I am sure there were some moments in our childhood when he simply scooted out of the room and let Mom take over, because what was going down was not something he wanted to get anywhere near.

Keep your head down, shut up, and wait for this one to blow over.

That's what I did. And every time one of my kids ever mentions her vagina for the rest of her life, that's what I will continue to do.

9

Having Children of the Opposite Gender

or My Mom DID Have to Deal with This Stuff

IT IS SAID THAT parents of children who are of the opposite gender are closer to them than parents of the same gender. Hence the term "daddy's girl" or "mama's boy" (though the term "mama's boy" also seems to have a negative connotation). I don't believe that this is true, particularly, as I am super close with both my steady, wonderful, weird mom and my gregarious, robust, and thoroughly weird dad. But it is something that I have in common with my mom. While I live in a home surrounded by women, my mom was in a home surrounded by gents. So while I am outnumbered today, she was outnumbered back in the 1970s and '80s, when I looked more like this:

I should start by saying that my mom is one of the kindest people that you could meet. She was born and raised in San Antonio, Texas, and grew up as Margaret Woelfel in a house full of German Texans. As if Texas isn't stubborn enough, my ancestral tree is also filled with plenty of German whimsy. My mom grew up quiet and smart and liberal, in a conservative house. She's the eldest of three; there's her sister, Marty, and her brother, George, too.

Anyhow, much as I am surrounded by ladies in my life, my mom was surrounded by fellas—my dad and us two boys. And we were a boyish lot, too. My dad watches football and actually any sporting event he can get his hands on. He bellows a constant stream of encouragement and insults at the TV during the game. My brother and I played many sports and were loud and boisterous, and when we got older in high school we became very interested in beer. We ate a lot, drank a lot, and told dirty jokes. In short, we were boys. However, we weren't all bad. We loved our mom and were respectful to her. We also know that she was the real power in the house. She was strict when she needed to be, and she was and is the person that almost all of her friends go to if there's a problem. She has a good head on her shoulders and nothing can faze her.

I understand to some point what my mom must have gone through with all of us boys in the house, as sometimes my wife and daughters speak a language that I do not fully understand. Vivian once looked at a possible new comforter for her bedroom and said, "Mom, I feel like it's competing with the wallpaper." Georgette quickly agreed, and Melissa almost fell over, being so excited that her girls wanted to discuss this very important event. Then, to be nice, they all asked me what I thought of the new comforter. As I stammered out a general approval, they went on to other things that I didn't altogether understand. Not to reduce us all to clichés, but once in a while, there are things that the opposite gender has a bit more difficulty understanding. For me, understanding the competition between comforters and wallpaper is definitely one of them. I haven't been left out in the cold winds of an isolated gender long enough to snap, though—and one time my mom was. And she did.

Let me explain. My father, brother, and I all have been known to wear baseball hats at any time, for any occasion. (I have since restrained myself.) We favor the Philadelphia Phillies, and my dad may have at any one time upwards of seven billion baseball hats in his closet. And Flynn and I would be tromping around with our dirty hats as well. I believe I have my hat situation under control now, and I believe Flynn wears hats only a few times a week, to places like the beach. My dad probably still wears a baseball hat every day of his life. My mom would gently mention to us that we could consider going hatless, and we would gently say yes and then continue wearing baseball hats every waking moment of our lives.

One day, when I was in my early teens, my dad, brother,

My brother on his graduation day. My dad, in a
baseball hat, is striking a playful pose.

and I were, of course, all wearing baseball hats. We were
pretty dirty. We were awful boys. We were talking about
sports. (By the way, everyone who works for Melissa's and
my company is female, and the other day I eventually had
to gently step out of the room when a discussion took a long,
long turn to Jennifer Garner's choice of footwear, and FYI,

everyone agreed that her sneaker choice was both comfortable *and* cute.)

Anyway, we were talking about sports and eating chili con queso, from my mom's recipe. It's kind of incredible, really, and it's so simple. I have to give you the recipe.

My Mom's Chili con Queso Recipe

One block of Velveeta

One can of chipotle peppers

One roasted poblano pepper

Directions: Melt it all down and eat it with chips.

So we were eating this great chili con queso, and I saw that my mom was getting very antsy. I couldn't figure out what the problem might be, but she seemed fidgety, borderline agitated. She was looking at us all in our hats and she'd asked us all so very nicely to stop wearing them all the time, and something in her just snapped. She said, "This is just crazy."

I said, "What's crazy?"

She blurted out, "All of these hats are just crazy. I can't take it anymore."

My brother said, "What's the big deal? They're just hats."

My mom shot him a look and walked over to the coat tree, where we had a collection of novelty hats, including a witch's hat for Halloween and a sombrero my dad had picked up on some sort of adventure. She grabbed the sombrero and said, "You know what? Let's *all* wear hats. I'm never taking this hat off my head."

I took off my hat and said, "Mom, fine. I won't wear it. But I have hat head."

With stunning speed, my mom sprinted over to me and said, "Don't take it off. We're all wearing hats now." And then she jabbed me in the forehead with the brim of her sombrero. "Isn't this fun? Hats!" she yelled, and she jabbed me again. She walked over to my brother with a crazed look in her eyes, and she got right in his face and just stared at him. Then she yelled, "Hats!" right in his face and jabbed him in the forehead with the brim of her sombrero.

My dad said, "We've finally driven her crazy, boys. Be careful," and he started to slink away toward the living room. And my mom said, "Not so fast, mister. I am going to poke you in the head with my sombrero." And she walked over slowly to my dad, and she did it. She poked him in the forehead with the brim of her sombrero.

He said, "Okay, you feel better, hon?"

And she said, "You know what? I do. I really do." She wore the sombrero for at least the next three hours, and intermittently poked us hard in the head with the brim.

The message here is: Don't fuck with my mom. Also, hats can be fun, but they are not necessary.

I share something else in common with my mom. We are both quiet types who respond to stress with a certain quiet resolve. If my stress involves trying to cope when my daughter says she has an itchy vagina, my mom's stresses must have had to do with all the dirt and awfulness that came with a house full of us hat-wearing boys.

One Friday night we were having a party, and my mom was telling Cheri (remember her? She's the one who infamously told my dad that his "ball was out" of his shorts on a summer night in Carbondale) about how many hats we all wear in the house. She and Cheri immediately put on witch hats and drank a boatload of whiskey and wine as my mom talked Cheri through the madness. It was raining hard outside, and our sump pump was broken, so our basement was flooded with a few feet of water. The kids and the mostly inebriated adults went on our basement stairs to take a look.

I was sitting there with Cheri in her witch hat and she was laughing and saying, "Peg never even drinks! Isn't this fun?" And that's when my mom jumped into the water and started swimming in the basement. It's a mark of how much respect she has among the group of friends that there was very little judgment thrown her way after she made her decision to go swimming in basement water. In fact, I believe there was some solemn applause. I hope that I am so well respected among my friends that if I ever choose to cut loose, put on a witch hat, and swim in the basement, I do not receive derision or judgment . . . but rather a few laughs and gentle applause.

Someday the sheer amount of ladies that I live with might cause me to act out, as my mom did lo those many years ago. My version of this freak-out involves me in a full football uniform rushing into a room where something particularly girlish is going on and screaming, "FOOTBALL! FOOTBALL! WE ALL LOVE FOOTBALL!"

The only small issue with my testosterone plan is that I am not much of a football fan.

10

Parenting the Parents

or The Art of Waking Up Your Dad When
He Falls Asleep on the Can

MY MOM AND DAD'S favorite hangout when I was a
kid was The Pinch Penny Pub. We spent a lot of time
there, usually Friday and Sunday nights. All the families of
my parents' friends would go to the bar, and the owner, a
likable Greek dude named Frank Karayiannis, would make
pizza for the whole gang of us. The adults would gab and

---

drink booze and the kids would run around. Everyone was a winner. We all had a blast.

One of my father's hobbies at that time was drinking whiskey. He once famously referred to Jameson's Irish whiskey as feeling like "Jesus pissing down your throat." Dad has a way with language. Being an English professor and all.

On Sunday nights at the pub, my dad's oldest friend, Joe Liberto (who moved from Philly to Carbondale to go to school at SIU with my dad way back when), would play piano in a jazz band called Mercy.

Anyhow, Mercy was a really good band, with a good sound, and the sax player, Buddy, could wail on the sax and also the flute. Sometimes he even played percussion on this little wooden box shaped like a fish that made a tap-tap-tap sound. I loved that band. Joe was incredibly talented, and he would play extended improvisational solos where no one knew what he was going to do next—but in the end he always brought it back around to the melody. I also loved them because they would play "Linus and Lucy" from *Peanuts* for me when I asked. And when I got older, they'd play the theme song from *Romancing the Stone*, and Buddy would bust out his sweet flute and he'd just really *get there*. Good times.

So Dad was enjoying his whiskey hobby, and the rest of us were enjoying Mercy. These were good nights at The Pinch Penny. However, for some reason during this time (whiskey?), my dad started to fall asleep on the toilet. The pub had a small bathroom. There was one urinal and one stall, and a lot of people—so if someone took a long time in there, it really gummed up the works.

I don't know if my dad was consistently drunk or consistently tired (I'm guessing a combo platter), but I do know that at least once a week it became my job to go wake him up as he slept on the john. Someone would walk up to Kelly, my mom and dad's Chicago friend who owned the bar at that time (Kelly into the bar with Frank), and whisper something to him. Kelly wouldn't miss a beat, and he would good-naturedly yell, "Ben! Get your pop outta the john!" I'd walk in, past the person invariably at the urinal, kick open the stall door, and find my pop snoozing away. I'd nudge him, and he'd say, "What? What's happening?"

Then he'd see me and say, "Hey, buddy," as casual and breezy as if we were having a quick beer together (not that I was old enough to drink beer, but you get what I mean).

"Pop, you're asleep on the toilet again." With that, my dad would look down at himself, smile, and say, "So it would seem." I'd step out, he'd splash some water on his face or whatever he needed to do to get himself together, and go back out toward the band as if nothing had happened at all.

I am careful with any and all of my bodily functions. I choose to believe that I am part robot, and that I neither need fuel nor create waste. I certainly did not get that from my dad.

A few years later, when I was attending the University of Illinois at Urbana-Champaign (sister cities, gang!), my dad came out drinking with my friends and me one night. For me that seemed like a normal thing to do, as my dad and I were so close, and I think our comfort level with the hanging-out situation rubbed off on my friends. Before long, nobody thought it was weird that my dad was drinking pitchers with us, especially since he was paying. Anyway, at the end of the night we went back to my friend Brian's apartment. Brian lived in a fun building filled with college students, where everyone was always having parties. A group of pretty girls from upstairs were there this evening, and they and every-body else at the party loved my dad. A fun parent with a beard and a quick laugh, who's drinking cheap beer with them— what's not to like? I think he even bought some more bot-tles of booze for the party. He was definitely a big hit. A girl who I was interested in but was unfortunately named Jamie Butts was there, and I was killing it that night with some of my patented "comedic dancing." This was at a point when I was deeply into a comedic dancing phase, an unfortunate phase that many young comedians go through in which they feel that jerky, strange movements on a dance floor will get a laugh. Sometimes these frenetic and crazed movements do elicit laughter, and unfortunately will lead to years more of comedic dancing until all of a sudden the comedic dancer hits thirty or so and realizes that he is a big, stupid dummy, and that all of the laughs were for the wrong reason. Or at least that happened for me. Perhaps other comedic dancers can keep it going longer, but I certainly could not. Anyhow, I fervently believed that if I could dance funny enough, ladies would pay attention to me. Meanwhile, moody guys with awesome abs did not need to dance around like clowns for attention. Those fuckers just stood around like bricks, and still got girls. Those guys all drive cool boats today, and they never had to dance for 'em. But I digress.

At some point the booze got a hold of me and I lost track of both Jamie Butts and my father. When I realized that my pop was nowhere to be found, I panicked a little, and started looking for him. Someone told me that he had gone upstairs to find a bathroom. I knew what that meant. This was not good. Horrified, I ran upstairs to the pretty girls' apartment to stop it all from happening.

I was too late. Jamie Butts grabbed me. "Hey, your dad fell asleep in our bathroom while he was taking a shit. Can you get him out of there?"

He did. I did.

I never did end up going out with Jamie Butts, but God knows I tried. One time I even told her I was a big runner in order to spend more time with her. (I ran, but not, like, as a habit.) So Jamie and her pretty friends took me on a run and we ran *eight fucking miles.* I had never run more than three miles in my life. I was the only guy in the pack, and all of these pretty girls ran eight miles like they were walking down the street to the coffee shop. I somehow made it through sheer fear of embarrassment, and pretended that I was fine. Of course I couldn't move the next day. Such was the depth of my affection for Jamie Butts.

Someone told me that she eventually married a man named Roger Titsworth. If that is true, her name today is Jamie Butts-Titsworth. I don't know why, but I am desperate to believe this.

If this story doesn't describe the depth of the father-son relationship, I don't know what does. You have to really love your dad to go into the bathroom of the girl you have a crush on and yank him out. A lesser son would have just walked away. And a lesser father wouldn't have been in that bathroom in the first place. I think it says a lot about my dad that he came to hang out with me in college, to meet my friends and see what my life was like at school. I also think it says a lot about my dad that he is so cool that no one batted an eye at the old guy hanging around. Except for when he passed out in the john.

I can only hope that the girls like me that much when

they are in college. Chances are that scenario won't repeat itself—it is different with fathers and daughters, and things are just different now in general. But what's important is the bond, the love that is so strong that you'll go into the john and wake up your sleeping dad. And forgive him for ruining your chances with Jamie Butts (though let's be honest—it was probably the comedic dancing that did me in).

———

11

Admit Your Faults

or Don't Mutilate the Chocolate Bunnies

MY DAD LOVES CHOCOLATE. He loves it like a sculptor loves his clay. It's a well-known fact all throughout the greater Carbondale area that my father is a chocolate fiend. His desire knows no bounds. Dark, milk, with nuts, without. It is all the same to him. Delicious. Quite recently my dad was staying at my house in Los Angeles, and he revealed that he'd gone to sleep with chocolate pretzels in his pockets. You know, just in case the obsession struck him at around 4 a.m. He didn't want to have to walk to the pantry.

My brother was a smart cookie growing up. He was active

---

in many clubs, always taking a school trip to Washington, DC, or Colonial Williamsburg or someplace like that. One year, the German Club was planning a trip to Germany. In order to raise enough money to go, Flynn was supposed to sell a bunch of chocolate bars. I believe the idea was that you had to sell somewhere north of 20,000 candy bars. Now, the German Club never went, because it costs a lot of money to get to Germany and nobody could sell the 20,000 candy bars needed. Kids would walk around the halls of our high school with these cardboard boxes that each contained twenty candy bars, and they'd sell them to the kids and teachers until everyone got sick of them. Or kids would take the boxes of chocolate to their parents' jobs and try and dump some product there.

My brother had another tactic. He did nothing. He just put the box filled with twenty chocolate bars on the dining room table. Then he waited.

It wasn't long before my dad passed by and saw that box on the table. "Ah, jeez," he said. Then he steeled himself and said loud enough for my brother to hear, "Not this time. Not this time, son."

Then my brother and I went to school. When we got home from school that afternoon, the box was short three candy bars. Three crumpled one-dollar bills lay on the dining room table next to the box. "Hey, guys," my dad said. "I am ashamed." My brother just smiled and tidied up the cash next to the cardboard box. "It's all over, though, son. That's all the chocolate I'm going to have this week," my dad promised. You could hear the sadness in his voice. He was powerless over his addiction, and he knew it.

When we got home from school the next day, the crumpled one-dollar bills had disappeared from the table and had been replaced with a ten-dollar bill. I called out, "Dad?" There was a long pause. And then, from upstairs, I heard his voice call out, "I'm ashamed."

Flynn had him on the ropes. And like a prizefighter, Flynn knew how to finish. He left that box of chocolate bars right where it was, but opened the top of the box just a tiny bit so anyone passing by would see those delicious bars. It was evil in its simplicity. This was a Tuesday, and Tuesday night was margarita night at a restaurant my dad liked called Tres Hombres. As was his routine, my dad went and had his margaritas with his buddies, and Flynn, Mom, and I stayed home for dinner and some television. When we woke up the next morning, the box was empty and there was a twenty-dollar bill on the dining room table. The note beside the empty box simply read, "I'm ashamed." Flynn had won the fight.

Easter was one of my favorite holidays when I was a kid. My oldest daughter loves it too, so that is a nice connection we share. Back then my mom would buy chocolate Easter bunnies from the grocery store and place them high on top of the refrigerator so that my brother and I could not get to them before Easter Sunday. She obviously put them up there to make sure Flynn and I wouldn't eat them, but she had another reason, too. She hoped that by putting them in the open, my dad wouldn't eat them in secret, hiding in shame. If he wanted to eat them, he'd have to do it in full view of everyone. She hoped that he was mortified enough by the very notion of this that he'd restrain himself.

One Easter when I was about ten years old, I woke up excited that the big day had arrived. It was Easter Sunday, and that meant chocolate. I wasn't as obsessed with chocolate as my dad, but I did love a chocolate Easter bunny on Easter Sunday. That day, we had some breakfast, after which I asked, of course, "Can we have our chocolate Easter bunnies now?" My mom smiled and went to get the Easter bunnies down from the top of the refrigerator. There was a box of five small chocolate Easter bunnies, all standing side by side. She put them on the dining room table and as she did so, she noticed something strange.

"Steve!" she shouted. I looked down and I saw what had upset my mother. Someone had eaten the ears off all five of the chocolate Easter bunnies.

"Yeah?" my dad said as he walked in, easy breezy, already planning his defense.

"Steve, did you eat the ears off of all these chocolate bunnies?" He looked her right in the eyes and sincerely said, "No, dear. I did not. Probably one of the kids did."

In quick unison my brother and I yelled out that this was completely untrue. My mom did not believe my dad for a second anyway, so we really didn't need to defend ourselves.

She gave him a look that said a million things in its severity and he knew the jig was up.

"Okay," he said, "I'm sorry. I ate the ears off of the bunnies. I couldn't help it." I was pretty sad that all of the bunnies had been defiled in this way and I said, "Dad, couldn't you have just eaten one whole bunny and left the rest for us?"

He looked at me and said, "You know what? That would

have been a good idea. I didn't think of that." My brother thought for a second and said, "That's not true. You ate all the bunny ears because they're the best part."

My dad had a look in his eye that was part defeat and part pride in his oldest son. "The ears are delicious," he admitted.

What I've taken from my dad's love of chocolate is this: It's fine to love chocolate, but it doesn't have to be a secret. Admit your faults. Kids can smell it on you if you don't. Also, when you are getting chocolate for your kids, get a backup stash of chocolate for yourself just in case you get a craving.

Admit what you have done and take the consequences. People are quick to forgive; they just need to know the score. And that's what I'll do with my kids: I'll own up to the things I've done wrong and look to move forward.

Also, I have done extensive taste tests, and although I cannot provide a scientific explanation, I can say with certainty that the ears on chocolate bunnies are indeed the best part.

12

All Hail the Road Warrior

or Being Grateful for What Matters

WHEN I WAS IN fifth grade, and my dad was in the midst of his ten-year stint of being marginally employed, and my mom was still our family breadwinner, my dad focused on writing his novels. (He hated editing; when they were done, they were done.) In between slaving away at the typewriter, he was Mr. Mom. Or rather, all-hands-on-deck dad—he took my brother and me to school and soccer practice, did the pickups too, the whole deal. My mom did more than her fair share of these parental duties, for sure, but I can safely say I grew up with a dad who was very comfortable staying home for a while and pitching in with the kids, which was pretty rare in the '80s.

There were two middle schools in Carbondale. One was on the richer side of town, which my father scoffed at. He was certain all the parents of these rich kids were Republicans, you see. He has always been a liberal, a borderline communist if I'm honest. He would often murmur, "We should take all the politicians outside and shoot them in the street." To which my brother or I would say, "Jesus, Dad." And he would bark, "We don't have to kill them! We just have to scare them. Goddamn crooks."

There was also a school on the other side of town in our district. This is where most of the poorer kids went. This is also where a lot of the minority kids went. This is where I went to school, and I really liked it. I shared my father's disdain for the "rich school" and thought my teachers were better and that I was getting a better education right where I was.

Being so righteously indignant served us well in that, well, we basically had no money. My dad made no money. My mom made enough to pay the bills. There just wasn't much left over. But when my dad decided he needed a car, this presented a bit of a problem. One day, with no one's permission but his own, my dad went out and paid $120 for the biggest piece-of-shit car in the history of this universe. It was a giant brown boat, rusted out, and the trunk had to be tied down with a piece of rope. It was literally hell on wheels. My dad had an immediate fondness for it. He named the beast "Road Warrior."

This is not the actual car. The "Road Warrior" was much more of a piece of shit.

My brother, as he often was when faced with many of my father's decisions, was surprisingly serene. He immediately accepted the Road Warrior into our family and gladly accepted rides to and from school in that awful shit-can. One time on the way to soccer practice, my brother calmly mentioned to my father that the Road Warrior was on fire, and suggested that they pull over and pour water on the engine. Done, and done. And off they went.

I was less fond of the Road Warrior. I was weak, what can

I say. I didn't want to face the fact that we didn't have a ton of money, and that is what the Road Warrior reminded me every time I looked at its evil face. I shared my boom box with my brother, and that was shameful enough.

The simple fact was that I didn't want to be seen in that car. I insisted that my father drop me off a block or more from school. He and my brother found this very funny, but they would oblige. They would wait for me to get to the school drop-off point, and then drive by honking and waving, yelling out, "'Bye, Ben! Nice driving with you!" And off they'd go to the junior high school in that demonic piece-of-shit car.

One day we were running late to school. I blamed it on the Road Warrior, of course. I have no definite recollection as to the actual chain of events, but I am reasonably sure that my dad's stupid fucking car took a lot of time to start up. Whatever the case, I was going to be late, and my dad informed me that he was going to have to drop me off at the actual drop-off point. Where all my friends would see. And everyone would know that we were poor.

I told him I'd sprint. I pleaded. I begged.

My dad listened to his ten-year-old son for a while, his son who was basically whining, and shaming him about the fact that his car was a piece of crap and we had that piece of crap because he didn't have a job. But my dad didn't get angry. He just said, "Buddy, it's just a car. It's not a big deal." What is or is not a big deal is something that I struggle with.

I ducked down in my seat, pretending that my father was driving my brother around in the backseat, chauffeur-style. The illusion was blown when, at the drop-off point, my dad opened the door and said, "Have a good day, buddy," and I was forced to exit the front seat of the Road Warrior. Kids stared at me like I was exiting a gold-plated limousine, except the opposite. None of them said much, but to my recollection, roughly two hundred kids stood and stared at me and all simultaneously thought, "Ben Falcone drives around in *that piece of shit*?" Or at least that is what I thought they thought.

I silently walked to my class. I was ashamed because my dad drove around a piece-of-shit car. And I was even more ashamed that I was ashamed of my dad's car.

My school was fairly rough-and-tumble. I avoided fights by telling jokes and by belonging to as many groups as I could, without fully committing to any of them. By blending in and being generally amiable and sort of funny once in a while, I avoided most of the violence that could be perpetrated upon my beautiful face. There was an undisputed king of the school, and his name was Kerry. How the king rose to power with a girl's name was a question I could not answer, and it was not in my best interest to inquire. What I did know is that if you could keep Kerry happy, you'd stay out of trouble, and there would be no violence against your (my) beautiful face.

The day that everyone saw me get dropped off at school in a car that was too shitty to even put in a movie about a shitty car, I somehow found myself in a bit of trouble with a tough group of kids on the playground. Maybe I was trying to be funny and I took it too far? Maybe I was too quiet, and that was a sign of disrespect? I honestly don't remember. What I do know is that I was surrounded by two large boys and a really tough girl named Vernita who seriously *kicked ass*, and that one of the taller boys had just pushed me and said, "What are you gonna do about it."

I know that "What are you gonna do about it" as a phrase doesn't have a lot of great answers, unless you are really good at fighting. I was not really good at fighting, so upon hearing those words, I began to get sweaty, the world looked shimmery—and in a dreamlike state I realized I was about to have horrible violence perpetrated upon my beautiful face. I was just hoping Vernita didn't get too involved. She was by far the toughest kid in school, and could have easily been the king instead of Kerry, but I think she didn't want to commit to the administrative responsibilities. I just stood there waiting for the really tall kid to hit me.

Suddenly, Kerry rushed over. I thought, "Holy shit. Now

Kerry wants in. This is going to be incredibly unpleasant, but at least this is *news*." I mean, if Kerry wanted to fight me, everyone in the school would be talking. It wouldn't be good for me, physically, but it might raise my social standing a little. So I prepared myself. To my surprise, Kerry didn't take a swing at me. Instead, he got in the tall kid's face and said, "Ain't nobody gonna punch Benjy. You understand?" Relief flooded my body like sunlight on a field of daisies.

Then Kerry composed himself and said, "Benjy's too poor to beat up. You see the car he drives? Damn. Let the little man be." The tough kids all looked at me, and there was one very clear look they all shared. That was the look of pity. They all pitied me because of my dad's horrible piece-of-shit car. The mean kids unclenched their fists and went to go look for a game of kickball, a game in which Vernita would inevitably kick the ball about three fucking miles every single time she came up to the plate.

I was off the hook. The Road Warrior had saved me from a beating. No two ways about it, I was relieved. The king of the school had just spared me an ass kicking. But the whole incident made me think a bit more deeply about my family's financial situation, too. I mean, I guess we *were* kind of poor. My dad drove a car that cost $120. He was unemployed. My mom was a social worker. The only place we went out to dinner at was literally named The Pinch Penny Pub. Not what you usually read about in *Forbes* magazine. But we had enough to eat and we had clean clothes and we were a happy bunch. We laughed all the time. My dad was larger than life. My mom endured a house full of males with a smile on her face, most of the time. So what, we had an embarrassing car. My dad was right. It was not a big deal at all.

What my dad really taught me with the Road Warrior is that material things don't matter. He didn't give four shits if he had a bad car, and neither did my brother. Which must mean they were less materialistic than me and somewhat better people. To this day, my dad only cares that everyone is healthy and having a good time and truly believes that the rest of life is gravy. I decided that from that day on, I would no longer be ashamed of the Road Warrior. If it was good enough for my dad and my brother, it would be good enough for me.

Luckily enough, the Road Warrior completely disintegrated less than a month later. I don't remember the exact cause of its demise. It probably caught on fire, and laughed an evil laugh as it died in a fury, and then floated off to meet the devil.

As an adult, I have had long stretches during which I had no money whatsoever, and points in life where I've done pretty well financially. One of my biggest fears is that my kids will grow up to be jerks because they've never had to ride in a Road Warrior. But I can't just go out and buy an evil car that catches on fire to teach them a life lesson, can I? I guess I could. But that wouldn't really work in the context of their lives, or mine at this point, would it? I guess I just have to trust that our girls are good people and hope that they care about people more than stuff, remaining the loving and great girls they are.

ACTUALLY: You know what? Fuck it. Right when they go to high school, I'm buying a Road Warrior. Just a real beastly shitbox of a car. And I am going to drive them to school in it every day. Vivie, Georgie—you'll thank me. I promise.

Maybe that was my father's plan all along?

13

How to Be an Inspiration to Young Athletes

PS: Maybe Skip the Mimosas?

I **PLAYED SOCCER AS** a kid, every Saturday morning in the fall. I still remember the smell of crisp autumn air as I laced up my cleats and put on my shin guards. I was so excited to play in those games. Soccer was a big deal in Carbondale. We were a university town (Southern Illinois Salukis, y'all!), and we came to soccer earlier than a lot of the country. Back in the early '80s when I was playing, there was a giant boys' league and a big girls' league, with kids from ages seven to fourteen playing. Pretty much every kid in town played in those soccer games, and they were always the highlight of my weekend. I played offense and made up for my lack of speed or aggression with a "nose for the ball." I liked to dribble down the sideline and pass it to the center forward, who would try to sail it into the goal. When it all worked according to plan, it was like a dream.

Whether the plan worked or not, the joy of the game was getting the ball down the sideline and looking for that perfect pass. When I was in junior high school, I had a coach named Morris Lamb, who was a down-to-earth nice guy. He wasn't a professional coach or anything, just an interested dad who fell into coaching. I'm not sure how much he, or any of us, knew about soccer, but I know that I got some of my first big laughs from a group of my teammates by impersonating him. When he yelled to the team from the sidelines, he sounded more like a play-by-play announcer than a coach. *"Down the sidelines, Benny! Down the sidelines!*

Shoot, Benny! Shoot, Benny! Score, Benny! Ooooh, Benny! Oh, Benny. Next time. Back on defense! Nice try, Bennnny!" The fact that he never got mad about me impersonating him is a testament to how nice he was. Like Morris Lamb, my dad fell into coaching, too. But he got involved in my soccer career long before Mr. Lamb.

My dad was a coach for my team when I was pretty young, maybe ten years old. Our team was actually pretty good. We were too lazy to create a team name. Take a look at our killer uniform. (Apparently, American kids of the '80s played soccer in jeans?) The kid on the far left is named Johnny Graubner, and he was our secret weapon. I would feed that hungry beast and he would crush the opposition mercilessly in his bell-bottom blue jeans.

As I've mentioned, my mom and dad were part of a very fun group of parents. We were a part of the group of four families (not like the mob) that would meet at The Pinch Penny Pub for pints and pizza on many an Illinois evening. This is the same group who met at the soccer fields on Saturdays. These parents supported their kids always, and they were quite active in the community. They were also a funny, smiley group, and I was happy they belonged to me. I felt like part of something special.

My brother always hung around at my games too—he liked soccer, but was more of a basketball enthusiast. He sometimes helped my dad out with coaching duties, but mostly Flynn was there to lend his support. One season in particular, we couldn't be stopped. It was a winning season all around. And on this particular Saturday, it was the championship game. Excitement was even higher than usual.

My parents and their friends, Dan and Judy, Joe Liberto, the Finnegans, the Kellys—they were all there, whether they had kids on the team or not. This was *a big game,* and our reputation was on the line. Bragging rights at The Pinch Penny were at stake, and they were damn well going to support our team.

Now, someone decided, and to this day no one has confessed, that the best way to prepare for a game of such importance at eleven o'clock on a Saturday morning was to make mimosas. Or maybe it was mojitos. It was some kind of sweet boozy concoction that starts with an *M* and ends in a hang-over.

And my dad, needing to be as prepared as he could be, had several of these drinks that began with an *M* as we kids warmed up. Maybe we dribbled between cones. I probably just pretended to stretch my hamstrings. (I hated stretching. Still do!)

It was about one minute to game time. The referee was on the field, looking things over, getting set for the epic match to come. The opposing team, the best team in the league (besides us), was gathered by their coach, Courtland Munroe, who just so happened to be my dad's heart doctor. My dad once accidentally ran over Mr. Munroe's mailbox, but that was an accident and was unrelated to our teams' rivalry.

My dad was teetering a little bit as he called us in for a little pep talk. "Boys," he said solemnly, "this is the big game. We've been waiting a long time to have another crack at Court's team over there." (We had lost to them earlier in the year, and that defeat didn't go down easily.) "But today is our day. I want you to remember that you're playing together *as a team*, and that I'm proud of you all. It's been my absolute pleasure to be your coach this year."

My dad looked at us all proudly, and he went silent for a second. And then he took a deep breath and screamed, "Now kill those motherfuckers! Kill those motherfuckers! Kill them!" He started pumping his fist and screaming, "Yes! Yes! Yes!" I think he was expecting us all to join in the chant, but we were stunned into silence. Dan Cross, a nice kid who was our best player and later went on to play for the University of Florida basketball team, looked up at my dad and said, "Mr. Falcone, I'm not comfortable with swearing." Dan's parents weren't part of the Pinch Penny crew, you see.

It's one of the very few times I have ever seen my dad look uncomfortable in his life. He was momentarily at a loss for words. But only momentarily. "Sorry, Dan. Umm . . . point taken." Then my dad looked at the rest of the team, overcome with raw emotion. "Team. I'm asking you . . . I'm begging you . . . Let's get out there and *Kick. Some. Ass!*"

We lost. Either 2–1, or it could have been 3–2. It doesn't matter. What my dad showed me that day is that it's not whether you win or lose, it's how you prepare the speech before the game.

Vivian plays soccer now, which she really enjoys. Georgie is going to start playing soon too, and judging from how ferociously she plays in the backyard, she should really play defense, and I recommend that players on the other team stay out of her way. Vivian is going to start softball soon too, which

I am delighted about. I liked soccer, but baseball was really my favorite. I don't like to talk about it, but I was pretty good. Made some all-star teams, you know. No big deal. For one of those all-star games, my brother bought me a new bat. And no kidding, in my first at-bat, I hit my first and only Little League home run. For my second at-bat, I whacked it off the fence in right-center field. I heard my dad screaming, "Go for two!" so I did. So what if I was thrown out at second base by at least ten feet. I never said I was fast, and it still technically counts as a single. I don't know why we got off subject discussing how I hit a home run in Little League—you know, I usually don't bring it up.

The point is, I probably won't have a bunch of mimosas with my friends before my daughters' next big game, whether it's softball or soccer. But I will show up to every single game. I'll bring friends and I'll support my kids. I'm into sports, just like my dad. And if our team loses, the opposing coach better guard his mailbox. That's all I'm saying.

This picture was *not* taken the day I went 4 for 5 with a home run and two doubles. That day *did* happen, though I don't usually bring it up.

14

Admit When You Have Said, Done, or Cooked Something Wrong

or The Apology Fish

WHEN I WAS A kid, from time to time my parents would argue. If the argument got deep enough, my dad would turn beet red and yell something smart like, "For the love of Christ!" Then he'd slam the door and storm out of the house. He would walk around the neighborhood for a while, maybe twenty minutes, and then come home and inevitably say he was sorry. My mom was quiet but firm in her convictions (it helped that she was usually right) and my dad knew when to fold. Flynn and I generally stayed out of the fray, but one time I sided with my mom in some sort of disagreement, and I secretly flipped my dad off as he walked away. My brother caught me.

SIDE NOTE/INSIGHT INTO MY PARENTS' MARRIAGE: My parents did not fight often—please don't get the wrong impression. My mom and dad have a great relationship, albeit a somewhat unusual one. One example of how unusual can be seen in this little story:

My mom is originally from Texas. As a graduate student in Illinois, she would go back and forth between there and Texas, where she visited her parents. During one of Mom's trips to Texas, my dad was left alone in Illinois. At this time, they were only dating, but my dad suddenly became convinced that they should be married at that very minute. So, my dad hitchhiked from Carbondale, Illinois, to San Antonio, Texas. I imagine that this journey took two days or so. Eventually, he got to my grandparents' doorstep in San Antonio and asked my mom to marry him. Her answer was "not right now." It didn't matter to my mom that my dad had spent the last two days hitchhiking across many states to pop the question. When I ask why it all went down like that, my mom smiles, gets a far-off look in her eyes, and pretends to not have heard the question. One day a few years later she did say yes, and now they are happy. They laugh a lot and enjoy each other's company. Whatever makes something work is not something to mess with, it's something to enjoy.

Once when I was probably fifteen years old (Flynn was off to college at the University of Chicago, smarty-pants that he is), my parents had an argument that was a little more serious than the average. Whatever my dad had done was bad enough that he felt he should make an elaborate apology to my mother, more than just a simple "I'm sorry." I should mention that my mom is a calm, caring lady, and not prone to anger, so the situation here, whatever it was, must have been pretty bad. And Dad knew it. He was going to have to go in pretty major with the apology this time. But what to do? Naturally, he chose to make my mom an apology fish dinner.

My father is a man of action. He has trouble sitting still, which is a trait I have inherited. As I write these stories, I type on a laptop, changing locations constantly, inside and outside, because somewhere deep I believe that if I stay in motion I'll stay safe. It's probably why my dad and I both love to take walks. Sitting still invites the demons. Getting on the move is the only way to ensure your happiness and keep darkness away.

Because my father has had a million part-time jobs, it turns out that he is a hell of a short-order cook. He makes a mean club sandwich in a startlingly short amount of time. He makes omelets that are tasty and fast and usually feature an exotic vegetable. So, in order to make up for his transgression, and to put his skills to work, he decided that he should make my mom a fancy dinner that would prove his love and show just how sorry he was.

So my dad got busy. He knew my mom was coming home from work soon, and time was wasting. I was informed that we were having fish for dinner. I was fifteen and am from the Midwest, so I was not exactly thrilled. But I sucked it up because I knew my dad must have really messed up royally if he felt the need to cook an apology fish. Fish is fancy. Fish is for company. And holidays. And clearly, for apologies when Dad really pisses Mom off.

So my dad was now banging around in the kitchen, frozen fish was being defrosted, and I think maybe bok choy had appeared on the cooktop. It actually smelled pretty good.

But then, my dad started telling me a story, as he is wont to do. He's a great storyteller, and he had been standing still for too long and gotten bored with cooking this fish. So he started telling me a story about the old days back in Philly, probably. Maybe about the time he went walking in the wrong neighborhood and he and his brothers got into a rumble, which it seems like they probably won. Someone in the story got hit with a car antenna. Maybe? Or the story could have been about a play he was currently involved in with his community theater. He did lots and lots of plays back then. He loved the stage. It doesn't really matter what the story was. The fact is, the story was a lot more interesting than the apology fish dinner that he was cooking.

The front door opened and my mom came in. She gave me a hug, as she always did. My dad called out, in a booming and gallant voice, "Hey, babe! I made you dinner!"

"Oh . . . okay," my mom said. I could tell she was hesitant, and also still a little bit annoyed with my dad. I was thinking that the dinner might not wipe away all of Dad's sins. But apology fish? At least the apology fish offered hope.

My dad, a tad too formally, invited my mom to sit down at the dining room table. Our dining room was very nice, but very simple. The only art in the room was a small piece of driftwood with a painting of a sailboat that adorned one wall that I believe we got in fucking Ocracoke. My dad hadn't decorated the table at all. No flowers or anything. That was simply beyond my father's scope. If I were a more astute kid, I might have suggested roses, but I was fifteen and had never had a girlfriend. What did I know?

My mom sat down and my dad poured her a glass of economically realistic champagne.

My mom started to thaw a little, as my dad was clearly putting on a show. She knew he was sucking up to her. And she was enjoying it. So, she asked him what was on the menu. "Fish," my dad answered, and I think I saw my mom suppress a look of fear.

My dad first brought out a plate of bok choy. They were lightly sautéed with some sort of Asian sauces. They are testament to how pretty exotic vegetables can be because on the plate, they are stunning.

Mom said, "Oh look. How nice," and I knew Dad was on the road to recovery. I made a mental note, tucking it away for the future. The way to win back your lady's favor, it seems, is to make her a nice, thoughtful dinner after a hard day's work. Then my dad reappeared, this time holding a dish with a bunch of grubby, gray, mostly raw-looking fish unhappily heaped upon it. "Here's the fish," he said proudly. That lunatic was so delusional with the thought of his own charm that he had the brass balls to actually be proud of that heap of garbage that was sitting on the plate.

Back to the fish. The fish had been just lightly sautéed, and it seemed like maybe he used a wok to prepare it. There was the faint smell of burnt ginger, and also the distinct smell of raw fish. I cut into the mealy gray mound on my plate, and the consistency was something south of Jell-O. As in, it was not fully firm. It was like Jell-O before it sets and is still liquidy.

My dad, it seems, had forgotten to actually cook the fish. He got wrapped up in his story and forgot to cook the goddamn fish. To his credit, he never let on that there was anything other than a delicious, beautiful entrée on our plates, ignoring the catastrophe that he was serving us.

I looked over at my mother as she cut into her slab, steeling herself for the inevitable.

Now we were all locked into a game of chicken. We each had our fork in the air, loaded with gray, smelly fish. This fish that had been hastily thawed, and then undercooked to a vile, gelatinous mess. And Jesus H. Christ, did I see hairs? Like weird little fish hairs? My mind started to race, thinking, "Where did my dad get this fucking fish? What is this strange beast he has served us?" And the only answer I can think of is Sam's Club. My dad loves Sam's Club, the members-only version of Walmart where you can buy things in enormous quantities. I bet he got this frozen shit on sale from Sam's

Club and now we were all going to have to eat this jellied raw fish and we were going to die. I looked at my parents. I knew goddamn well that I was not going to be the first one to take a bite of this hellfish. Upping the ante, my mom, in her most pleasant singsong voice, said, "Ooooh. Fish," staring at my dad and daring him to take a bite.

He squinted a bit, because he knew what was happening. He knew that he had just received a clear challenge. With her eyes, she had just said, "You cooked this shit. *You* eat it." He had no choice.

My dad brought the cartoonishly horrible fish up to his mouth, and he took a bite, and he slowly began to chew. The total lack of reaction was impressive, but it was clear to anyone within a hundred miles that the man was struggling not to gag. He kept at it, chewing with a calm detachment, though in the back of his eyes you could see that his soul was suffering. Until eventually, the fish material slid slowly down his throat.

I waited for him. My mom waited for him. And now I was thinking, "How did I get dragged into this? Why am I even here?" Because my parents were now in a detente. He'd had his bite and he was waiting for her to take hers. His apology dinner had turned into a disgusting food challenge.

Staring back and forth at them, feeling more and more panicked that once Mom took her bite (A) she would barf all over and/or (B) the duty would fall to me, I decided that

I must take action. I may be a coward by nature, but in this particular battle of wills, I had to do something. So I said, as diplomatically as I possibly could, "Dad, is this fish cooked, you know, *all the way?*" He looked at me and very slowly said, "I think so. Take a bite, and you tell me." Before I could stop the words from coming out of my mouth, I just said, "There's no fucking way I'm going to eat this, Dad."

My mom burst out laughing. So did I. My dad knew he had lost this fish battle and perhaps the fish war, but he soldiered on. "Peg. Just try it!"

"No way!" she shouted. And now my dad joined in the laughter, poking at the hellfish, saying, "It's not so bad, it's got some nice spices in there . . ."

"Then take another bite," I said, goading him on.

"Son," he replied, "there's no way that's going to happen." And with that my mom went into a fit of laughing so hysterically that I would have been afraid of her choking if she had eaten anything.

"He's afraid to eat it," she said.

"Of course I am," my father replied. "It's horrible. I wouldn't eat the bok choy, either. It tastes really strange."

What, you might ask, have we all learned from this tale of poor pescatarian preparation? Well, first of all, I hope to never do anything that requires me to make an apology-fish-dinner-type gesture to my wife. She's a good lady and she deserves the best I can do every day. But if I do make a mistake, and face it, all men do, I'll include my kids in the event, too. They'll help out, just like I did. I mean, if I hadn't been there, would my mom have eaten that fish? If so, my dad would have a whole lot more apologizing to do.

Just to be prepared, I have started working on my apology dinner menu:

First course: Caprese salad

Entrée: Filet mignon with potatoes and veggies or gluten-free pasta (Ka-fucking-boom!)

Dessert: Fruit in a fancy glass. Maybe a parfait kind of thing.

It's a can't-miss menu, guys. I really think I'm covered.

I would have rather eaten all of these terrible beasts
than the glop my father served on that fateful day.

15

High School— Let It Be a Time of Poor Choices

or Forgive Them, for They Know Not What They Do

FROM 1987 TO 1991, I attended high school. During these years, I looked like the picture on the next page.

Notice the fetching acid-washed blue denim jacket over the blue shirt, the unkempt eyebrows that are ever so slowly reaching for one another to form a glorious unibrow, the poorly executed haircut that comes to a strange point at

---

the top of my skull, and the required bad skin. Also please do not miss the detail that I am wearing BOTH a Led Zeppelin pin and a U2 pin. On an acid-washed denim jacket. I really needed to prove that I was a rockin' cool guy, I guess. One pin was not going to go far enough to establish my cred.

This photo is a classic case of bad teenage judgment. The reality is that I was a shy kid in high school who decided that he should make a statement for the yearbook photo. When I look at the photo now, I am justifiably horrified. But when I *took* that photo, I was convinced that I had done the first ballsy, totally cool thing in my life. Time teaches us all lessons, the most important of which is that we're all dipshits in high school.

FOR EXAMPLE, OUR CLASS motto, the chant that we would yell during basketball games, was "Sex and drugs are lots of fun, we're the class of '91." Catchy, yes, and even a strong rhyming couplet, but let's face it—pretty dumb. The worst part about our chant was that we knew we were easily topped by the lucky class one year older than us. They had coined the brilliant "Wine me, dine me, 69 me, we're the class of 1990"! To all high schoolers out there: you officially have to wait until the year 2090 to once again have the coolest chant in the universe. As you can imagine, the school administration was thrilled with all of the R-rated innuendo going on in our class mottos.

Where was my dad when I left the house the morning of picture day in high school? I HAVE NO IDEA. He conveniently DISAPPEARED. Which is exactly what all parents should do as their children make decisions in high school. I don't mean that once high school starts that most moms and dads should head to Key West, sending postcards and money every month or so only to return when the teenagers are finally ready for college. And then turn to their spouse and say, "Wow! That was so relaxing. I'm so glad we missed all of those mood swings and didn't have to deal with the drama of our kids not doing what we told them to do, choosing their friends over their families, sneaking out, breaking up with their boyfriends and then getting back together, wondering whether they are popular enough, trying to get into college and learning how to drive. I wonder how all that went?" I mean, that would be crazy. I don't plan on doing that. That's something I won't do when my kids go to high school, I swear! Because it's not something I've thought about at all, and I don't have an apartment on the beach picked out and a favorite bar to quietly write in, and I haven't already researched which deep-sea fishing boat I'll be the skipper of and I haven't got the departure and return dates already circled on huge calendars that I secretly keep in the garage. NO! Not at all! That would be crazy, and you have zero proof. You can't prove it. Also, I can do what I want; this is America. What I actually mean is that high school is a time when parents should disappear for the small stuff, and reappear for the bigger stuff. My father's belief, which I have also adopted, is that parents are responsible for attempting to keep their children from the truly big fuck-ups in life. The smaller stuff is the stuff that kids need to navigate for themselves. That's how kids figure out how the world works. That's how kids figure out who they really are. Give your kids room to grow, but drop the hammer when they are getting close to something that is galactically stupid.

My older daughter is a shy girl by nature, and I would do anything to protect her from the weirdness that high school is sure to throw her way. But I can't; that's just a fact. I won't be there at school with her every day and if I were, that would be terrible. For both of us. I don't want to relive that horror and she really doesn't want me there. All I can do is try to keep her away from the truly awful big decisions—drugs, drunk driving, acid-washed denim. I plan to disappear for the countless smaller decisions that she will make that will cause her to look back in horror thirty years later. (I will let Melissa deal with all of those smaller things, because I will be the skipper of a boat somewhere in a nameless Florida Key. But you can't prove it.) If my sixteen-year-old kid tells me that she wants to marry a guy named Zeke with no teeth who is a long-distance truck driver, for Christ's sake, I shall intervene. Fuck you, Zeke. It's not happening, buddy. But if she tells me she wants to color her hair pink or listens to shitty music or occasionally stays out too late, then that is definitely Melissa's domain. When I told my dad that I didn't want to go to the University of Illinois and would rather attend Southern Illinois University while living in a trailer with a friend of mine who partied a lot, he was rightfully mortified. He told me it was a bad idea, that I'd get a better education at the U of I.

And because he didn't nag me all the time about every little thing, I was more prone to listen to him on this one. Not that I did listen, not at first anyway. I heard him out but stuck to my guns, until my high school theater director, a fun and feisty lady named Mrs. Boyle, said, "Really? You're going to live in a trailer with your friend? Do you know that dorms are co-ed?" I admitted that I did not. "You are literally turning down a chance to live in a building with hundreds of pretty girls. What a shockingly dumb thing to do." While my dad had a good point regarding a better quality of education and life experiences, Mrs. Boyle had effectively narrowed in on my eighteen-year-old range of focus. I weighed the options—living either with a dude in a crappy trailer or in a dorm with hundreds of pretty college ladies. Needless to say, I enrolled at the University of Illinois later that day. Thanks, Dad, for trying. And thanks, Mrs. Boyle, for nailing it.

WHEN I WAS SEVENTEEN years old, I, like so many other teenagers before me, discovered the fun activity known as drinking beer at house parties. There would be a Pink Floyd record spinning, a bong doing the rounds, and a cooler full of cheap beer. I was still too nervous to smoke pot (though I got past my fears on that front later, and boy did I make up for lost time), but I would drink the hell out of a beer or two.

———

Since this was high school and I was still in my shy phase, I stayed pretty quiet throughout the night, off to myself, pounding beers. Being a novice drinker, I pounded one too many, which was of course when my crew had the bright idea that we should all head over to see *Back to the Future 2*. The sight of Michael J. Fox on that hoverboard was just too much for my beer-filled stomach and I got totally dizzy. I stumbled out of the theater and over to a pay phone to call my dad. I needed a ride home. He came to pick me up, and the minute I sat down in the car, I promptly threw up in the front seat of his beloved cherry-red CR-X.

This was a hammer-dropping moment, and I knew it. The next morning, my dad was pretty pissed, but he did manage to laugh. He told me he was glad I had called him instead of trying to drive, or driving with one of my friends who had been drinking. He also told me that it might be a good idea not to pound so many beers that I puke. And then he led me outside, where I had to clean and disinfect his beloved car that I had carelessly defiled.

I plan to take my dad's approach when the girls are in high school. If they make mistakes, I'll want to know if the mistake is illegal, something that can't be undone or will really mess up their lives in a major way for years to come (Zeke, I'm watching you). I will step in majorly. And if not, I will take Steve Falcone's approach: patiently explain why

———

the thing they have done was dumb, and nicely ask them not to do it again. And then hold them accountable. And that's pretty much it for high school, as far as I'm concerned. And if the issue at hand is just some teenage girl drama, a few tears and maybe a bit of a fashion disaster, well then, dear old Dad is keeping mum. That's all on Melissa. I'll be off fishing.

16

My Dad's Noises

(Oh Holy Shit, I'm Making Noises)

SINCE I WAS A little kid, my dad has made a series of noises. It's kind of a weird thing, so I'll try to explain it more clearly. Again, he is a remarkably loud man. He makes a loud yawning noise quite often, even when he's not really yawning. He'll sing a little snippet of a song, or he will sing the melody line of a jazz song, sort of making a saxophone noise. Or he will say little phrases if no one's around. Like, "Oh, baby." He loves the phrase "Oh, baby." There are some others, too. If there has been a little bit too much silence for my dad's taste, he has been known to say, "Ahh . . . Mungy,

mungy." I can't tell you what it means; I can only report that these are the noises that he makes. Constantly.

My brother has a theory, which I subscribe to as well. He says my dad's noises are "proof of life." The theory goes that if it gets too quiet in the house, my dad becomes concerned that perhaps people have forgotten that he is alive, so he makes a noise to remind them that he is a being who is in existence. Makes sense to me. These noises, it should be noted, have always driven me crazy. I find them alternately funny and annoying, and in the end, even though I understand and believe in my brother's theory, I just don't get the noises. I just don't.

This is the face of a man who can
make lots and lots of noises.

So the other day, I was in the shower. And I was trying to pretend that I was not naked, and I was grabbing some shampoo, and warm water was on my beautiful nude back. Out loud, out of nowhere, I said, "Oh, baby." The same way my dad says it, like it's the end of a hard day and you're finally taking a load off. So I did two things.

First, I immediately panicked. *Holy shit, I'm becoming my father.*

And second, I immediately forgave my dad for his lifetime of weird noises. Because I realized that there are one million weird things that I do that my kids can hold on to for the rest of their lives, and depending on their mood, they'll find them either lovable or annoying. One of the main bizarre things that I am told I do is that when things are happening quickly, when things are hopping, when we as a family need to get going fast . . . I start to move in slow motion. Perhaps it's the way I react to the stressful fact that we are five minutes late to school, or company is coming over and the house is a wreck, or I am late to a meeting with some sort of fancy person who can positively impact my career . . . I start to move like I'm in a world full of Jell-O. Is it a stubborn streak as if to say, "None of this is as important as it seems"? Melissa was the first to notice this wonderful feature that I possess, and now the girls, when things start moving too fast and I move into the deep recesses of my brain and begin to oh so slowly move across the kitchen toward the front door, will impatiently say, "Come on, Dad! Let's get movin'!"

What my kids don't know is that someday when they need to get moving quickly, they'll move in slow motion too, or maybe they'll make weird noises in the shower. Or do one of the thousand other weird things that have been handed down to them by generations of wonderful weird Midwesterners. Perhaps as a gift from Melissa, when they need to do something for work like memorize a lot of lines, they'll immediately grab a power drill and start installing shelves in a closet instead of sitting down with their script. There are many ways to make your kids weird, and we'll all do our fair share, I'm sure.

I can always hold on to the fact that to this point in my life, I have yet to fall asleep with chocolate pretzels in my pockets.

17

It's Okay to Let Them See You Sweat

but Sometimes I Sweat a Whole Bunch

WHEN I WAS IN my mid-twenties, my dad, my brother, and I took a trip to England and Scotland. We stayed with Flynn's best friend, Steve, who was working there for the summer, but this time Flynn and Steve did not get to go off and have all the fun, leaving me trapped in bird-watcher's purgatory. We toured the cities, we ate fish and chips, we drank tons of Guinness beer, and we took in the history all around us.

Toward the end of the trip, we took a train ride up to beautiful Edinburgh, Scotland, to go to a theater festival. (Note: We did not see a single play while there, but we did enjoy the many bars in the area and also I think we took a hike.) Sadly, the train was not air-conditioned. At around the halfway point in our journey, my dad began to sweat. Like, a lot. This was not a normal amount of sweat. Not normal at all. At first, I noticed that his forehead was moist and said to him, "Pop, you feeling okay?" He said, "You bet, buddy," and smiled. And just kept on sweating. Flynn took a look at my father's back and saw that he had completely sweat through the shirt he was wearing. I knew we'd been drinking Guinness on this vacation, and I was getting worried. "Pop—let's get you some water," I said. I immediately thought that we should take my dad to a hospital. I looked out of the train window and I saw lots of green fields, sheep, and stone fences passing by but very few hospitals. I began to feel anxious. My father seemed fine, except for the river of sweat pouring off of him. There had to be a reason for the sweat.

Flynn and I convinced my dad to go to the air-conditioned bar car, where (for around $60 of my dad's money) we got to sit in the cool air. My dad very slowly stopped sweating, and we very slowly decided that he didn't need to go to a hospital. I believe that he drank a bunch of water, at our recommendation, and a few glasses of Guinness, at his own. But, clearly something had happened to my dad. He got overheated. Maybe his blood pressure spiked. Maybe he was nauseous. I don't really know what it was, but I can tell you what it wasn't—nerves.

So here's something about me. My body does not want me to be an actor. My body begins to sweat whenever a camera is near. My face is fine; my beautiful face wants me to act and loves what I do. But my body loves to sweat and create wet patches on my clothing, causing me to tell the poor wardrobe people on set, "Hey, I'm kind of a problem. You might want to have two sets of everything for me." The characters that I play all tend to wear jackets that can cover their need to sweat through their clothes. Here's an example of how tricky my body can be, though. In *Tammy* I play an awful boss (Keith) to Melissa's character and we decided it would be funny if Keith sweat a lot. So no overshirt, no jacket, etc. But guess what? Since my body knew that sweating was acceptable, even good, it refused to do so. So I had to get sweat applied for that character. I digress, but the point there is that my body can be a real shithead.

Recently, at the beginning of a press junket for a movie, I was sitting on a chair jabbering on about the film, and I realized that I felt *pretty fucking moist.* I excused myself back to the changing area and realized that I had completely sweat through my shirt, exactly as my father had done on the train eighteen years before. *Holy shit.* I needed to go to a hospital. Something was wrong with me. Granted, I was wearing a sweater and there were hot lights, but this was an inordinate amount of wetness. It definitely had to do with nerves. I wasn't having a heart episode, contrary to my hypochondriac conclusion. And you know, I must enjoy the nerves in some way because I keep acting. I love acting. And when I'm doing a scene or a press junket, it's not like I can head over to the air-conditioned bar car and crush water and Guinness until my body stops raging like an oven on Thanksgiving. Luckily, our wonderful wardrobe person had a spare shirt and sweater with her that press day. I got through it. I will get through it again. And, I will sweat out another shirt, too.

Feeling nervous is something I battle as life goes on. As opposed to my father, I've always been a worrier, and now that I'm a dad, I have so much more to worry about. When I direct a movie, I feel nervous, because I don't want to let everyone on the set down who have paychecks depending on how well I do my job. And my wife and I have high standards for our work. But most of the nervousness I feel in my life is because:

1. I am getting older and hurtling ever closer to the "next phase," which is I think more or less scary for everyone.

———

2. I am a family man now, and I hope that I am doing a good enough job as a father and husband. I love my wife—and I know I am a lucky, lucky man. I adore my kids and I want them to have great lives, but there's only so much you can do to make that happen. The rest is up to them. Also, my kids are getting older. See 1.

3. Will the Phillies ever get a decent fucking bullpen?

A close cousin, but not exactly the same as nervousness, is anxiety. In addition to being nervous about a lot of things, I have many anxieties that I fight on a daily basis. Here is a partial list of what I feel anxiety about, day to day:*

1. I will get another concussion. (From putting on a hat, or from brushing my head against the leaf of a tree. We've been through this before.)

2. I either have food poisoning or am very close to getting food poisoning.

3. Something is wrong with my heart. (Not the loving part, the muscle part.)

---

* One of these is not really true. See if you can guess which one— we'll make it a fun game!

4. I am not really alive; I am just a brain in a barrel somewhere.

5. The Phillies will never get a power-hitting left fielder to replace the great Pat Burrell.*

Vivian and Georgie don't sweat too much so far. And that's a great thing, because I don't want them to feel the anxieties and pressures that I feel from time to time.

---

*   Also, the correct answer was 5. I know that someday the Phillies will get a great left fielder. We have a lot of great options in the minor leagues, and there's always free agency!

Recently, my dad had a snowball fight with the girls. And while a part of me didn't want people to hit others in the face and head with snowballs, I forced myself to really enjoy the moment. These are the great times of your life, the times when you should not be making a mental list of what might go wrong or how someone might get hurt, allowing anxiety to ruin a wonderful day. So I stopped writing that mental list. It was an awesome snowball fight. Georgie crushed my dad right in the face with a snowball. Man, she's got a great arm. To my knowledge, he did not suffer a concussion.

Do NOT mess with Flynn in a snowball fight. Good arm.

18

Music Makes the World Go 'Round

(This One Is Easy)

I **GREW UP IN** a house full of music. My parents had a
record player that we just *wore out*. We listened to a lot of
jazz (Miles Davis was the house fave) and a lot of Beatles.
The Beatles are the world's favorite band, so that makes sense.
There was some Cat Stevens in there, some Carole King,
James Taylor, and I personally loved the album version of *The
Hobbit* (I didn't have sex until later in life). There was music
on during dinner, during parties, while cleaning the house,

---

while decorating the Christmas tree. Our house was always just full of music.

I loved having music on during dinner. My mom made most of our meals (thank God; did you read that story about the apology fish?), and we would sit together as a family and eat dinner. There was never really a set time for us, but I always knew when it was getting close because the house would start to smell really good and my dad would throw on an album (later a CD). Jazz would usually start to play, but sometimes Flynn and I would pipe up with requests. While we were in high school we'd often have dinner listening to Led Zeppelin (but only the mellow stuff).

Music was our cue that it was time to relax and hang out as a family, and it's a cue that I still follow. I refuse to eat a meal without some kind of music on. When there's no music at dinner, I feel the silence weighing on me like a ton of bricks. Music makes the mood lighter. It makes the meal an "event" that we all gather for, not just some food on the table to plow through until we move on to the next thing. With some nice background jams on (that's right, I said "jams"), conversation flows more easily and everyone feels that stone-cold groove.

But here is possibly the most useful piece of parenting advice that you will get in this entire book. Ready for it? Here it is.

You don't have to listen to children's music. Ever. You just don't have to. No kiddie jingles, no kiddie music, no "Wheels on the Bus," no "Little Stars," no "Head, Shoulders, Knees and Toes"—no nothing.

You know why? Because they're kids and they don't know how to turn on the music player! Don't teach them! Remember, you are in control. My parents had music on all the time and were unaware that there was even children's music on this earth. So they listened to what they wanted to listen to and if we complained about something, they switched the album to something else that they liked. We never even knew kids' music existed. And we didn't miss it at all! We grew to love rock and roll and jazz and all kinds of great stuff. And when we were old enough to ask for music of our own, they bought it for us. And if they hated it, they just didn't play it at dinnertime.

Currently my kids' favorite album is the soundtrack to *Hamilton.* Yes, there are swear words on the album, but there are also a lot of great history lessons packed into those songs— am I right? They learn about the story of our VERY NATION! The kids listen to music that Melissa and I like. That's it. It's a win for everyone. Sure, the girls love Taylor Swift, but guess what? So do I, gang. *So the fuck do I.* She's a very talented young lady who writes a very well-structured pop song with catchy hooks, and, dammit, those lyrics sure get stuck in your head. So my advice is to listen to lots of music with your kids, and not that kiddie stuff either, and for the love of God, play music at dinner. Otherwise it's just a sea of forks clinking, and it makes me nervous. Plus, you'll give your kids a deep appreciation for music they can take into their lives. Good times call for good music, right? Choose the music that you play in the house, and listen to music with your family. Play music with them, if that's your thang. I personally play guitar, though I don't normally bring it up.

Apparently I used to really like to tan my legs.

19

Stop Feeling Guilty

Your Kids Are Never Really Bored

THE BIGGEST REALITY OF being a parent in the modern world is that we are constantly riddled with guilt. We have been led to believe that every day for our kids has to be an absolute Mardi Gras as well as an enriching educational experience. They need to be stimulated, but not too stimulated; they need to be around other children, and see lots of different kinds of environments, while also having a wonderful sensory experience that they will take with them into the world as they become worthwhile adults. And, they need to have a plethora of activities (but not too much of any one thing), both physical and intellectual, and eat a well-balanced, organic, gluten-free diet. Every single day, this is what they need. Feel like a failure just reading this? Yeah, me too. We're all failures.

All this pressure comes from a good place. It really does. We all just want the best for our kids, right? We want them to have it better than we did, to experience all the world has to offer. I sure do. And I feel guilty pretty much every single day that I am not doing enough for my girls, that I could show them the magic of the world if I only tried a little harder, if I was home more, if I was more creative, if I looked at my phone less, if I was less tired, if, if, if . . .

But here's the thing. Our parents didn't have to deal with this bullshit. They never felt guilty about whether or not they had taken us to see the latest Pixar movie or we had visited the new exhibit at the science museum. Maybe that's because they were just busy trying to pay the bills. Or maybe that's because there were no science museums back then. I don't want to go into some deep analysis of the current trend of the hyperactive helicopter parent. But I do know this—when I was looking to be entertained as a kid, my dad had one stock response, and it never, ever changed. It was, "Go outside."

These two words are the most awesomely powerful words

in a parent's lexicon. And they are in a way a cop-out, too, because they give you a time-out while you rest a minute. Because here's the other thing about kids needing constant fun, enriching times—this means you have to be involved in providing that. So of course, "Go outside" gives you a breather. But in another, more important way, they are the best words that any kid can hear.

I was an active kid in a different time. All my friends and I would ride our bikes everywhere, and I would play with my friends and friends of friends all day. But some days, everyone would be on vacation or just not around, and Flynn would be with Steve Merritt or some other cool older kid, getting a much-needed break from his younger brother. And my mom would be at work. So I'd be alone with my dad. I hated being alone, because being alone meant being bored. My dad was a fun guy and would play games for a while. But there was only so much he would want to do before he'd want to start reading a book or noodling around on a play he was writing. So I would get bored. So very bored. And when I was bored and my dad was busy reading or doing something I couldn't participate in, I would often whine, "Dad, I'm bored." And my dad would always say the same thing: "Go outside." I'd always beg him to come with me, because heaven forbid I go entertain myself. Dad would always appease me with "I'll be right out," which translated into "I'll be out anywhere between fifteen and forty-five minutes from now" or "You've got a brain in your head. Find something fun to do. You don't need me to do everything for you." Not that I actually heard it that way. But I'd head outside for a while and climb a tree or look at the sky or play in the yard or eat dirt, or whatever the hell it was that I did. Count pine needles. Feel the sun on my beautiful face. After what felt like an eternity or a minute (depending on my mood), he'd shuffle out and we'd play catch or take a walk and feel the sun on our beautiful faces. Sometimes he wouldn't come outside at all, and after an hour or however long it was that I'd been eating dirt, I would go back inside, somewhat annoyed, and say, "You never came out." And he'd look up from the book he was reading and reply, quite casually, "Ah. That seems to be true." He'd then close the book, stand up, and ask, "Want to shoot some hoops?" And we'd head outside and shoot hoops. He'd gotten some quiet time with his book, and I'd gone outside and pretended I was Han Solo, counted pine needles, or eaten dirt. I'd done the kind of imaginary play that is good for kids that I wouldn't have done if I'd immediately been able to force my dad to use his imagination instead of using mine. Kids need to make up their own games and worlds; it's how they learn how to be creative.

When my girls seem bored, I do often try and come up with a game that they'll like. One involves me as a giant who throws pillows at them, and every single time the game works out that they save their village and defeat the giant. Another involves me running after them until they turn into statues to stay safe. They laugh a lot at that one, and I get less hurt than I do playing the giant game. I'm not as young or as flexible as I used to be, you know?

But lately when they get bored or keep pushing for me to do something to entertain them, I will just look at them and calmly say, "Go outside." Somewhere along the line, I started to remember that the funnest games I used to play were the games I made up myself, or that my friends and I made up together. So I decided to try it with my kids, and it's changed my life.

Seriously, this is an excellent trick. You should try it. It will save you a lot of trips to the playground, Lego store, frozen yogurt place, children's museum, or petting zoo. Petting zoos are very gross places, so you are welcome in advance for this particular piece of advice. Listen, I try to do something really fun with my kids every day. We'll find a neat place to take a hike, write stories together, or run around, or I'll watch them ride their scooters in a particularly dangerous fashion. But once in a while I need a break to recharge and so do they. They need an hour to go outside and play in the dirt and make up games about fantastical worlds in which they are invariably in a management position. So their minds expand as they create and manage countless complex universes, and

I get to quietly sip coffee for a few moments. So it's really a win-win.

And after you've accomplished your tasks and had your alone time (coffee followed by a nap? So great), you can head outside too. See what your kids have come up with on their own. Take part in the game now that you're ready. You'll never be sorry you did.

20

Forget Counting Sheep When You Can't Sleep

One of the Many Reasons It Helps to Have a Sibling

MY BROTHER IS THREE years older than me. We have always been pretty close, I'm happy to say. Back in the day we were so close that we slept in the same room, lodged into bunk beds in my parents' two-bedroom house. I had the killer top bunk, and he was stuck in the boring bottom bunk. The fact that I rolled off my bed onto the wood floor several feet

---

below on a regular basis could not convince me that my bed was dangerous. It was the best bed in the world and I would not hear otherwise. Being that Flynn was the older of the two of us, you would think he'd get the top bunk, but the fact that he took the bottom and didn't complain shows just how cool of a guy he was, and is. This is what Flynn looked like as a kid:

Looks like someone you want to hang out with, right?

If there is a generalization to be made about the difference between my brother and me, it is perhaps that personality-wise, Flynn is a bit more like my dad (loud, fun) and I'm a bit more like my mom (quiet, weird—in a *good* way). Coincidentally, Flynn looks more like my dad, and I favor my mom. Eerie, right?

When I was ten years old I went through a bout of insomnia. Somewhere after my first very dangerous and terrifying hernia surgery, I found myself afraid of nodding off because I was worried I might not ever wake up. To help, my mom put a shelf next to my bed. That way, I could read my comic books until I was tired enough to fall asleep. Then, I could put my comics on the shelf and knock out for the night. The thing was, sometimes I'd put my book down and just lie there staring at the ceiling. A few scratches on the drywall seemed to make the perfect number 7. I'd look at it and think that maybe the room was lucky. But then I'd shut my eyes, and I'd feel unlucky and scared, and I'd be wide awake again.

On one of my wide-awake nights, my brother heard me shuffling around from his less cool bed.

"What are you doing?" I heard him say.

"I can't sleep."

"Sure you can," Flynn answered.

"I'm serious. I can't," I replied, sadly.

That's when my brother gave me some of his big-brother wisdom and a surefire cure for insomnia.

Flynn told me to think of my favorite thing.

I said, "I don't think I have a favorite thing."

"Sure you do."

"Okay," I said. "What is it, then?"

"I don't know. Maybe comic books."

I thought about this. "Oh yeah. That's my favorite thing."

"So think of Iron Man. You're Iron Man, okay? Blow shit up and beat up bad guys in your head until you go to sleep."

I tried it, and it worked like a charm. It still does. As I go to sleep, I think of something great (many times, I am still Iron Man, or I am Robert Downey, Jr., as Iron Man) and I nod off as I beat the hell out of various villains.

This is not a lesson that I have learned from my father, but I have used it already with my kids and so far, it's worked like a charm for them, too. And I'm glad that my girls have each other. As life rolls along, hopefully they'll give each other good advice, too.

21

Foster Political Ideas

or The Time I Was an Asshole for Halloween

CARBONDALE IS THE HOME of Southern Illinois University, which is a party school. There's an area near the campus not far from my parents' house called "The Strip," where all the college kids go to hit the bars and get loaded. These bars are not fancy, but they serve cheap booze and are within walking distance of the dorms, so they are well patronized. Outside of these excellent establishments there used to be a man named Winston who operated a bagel

---

cart during the late evening hours. He'd offer the drunken college kids leaving the bars a bagel with cream cheese for two dollars. Other schools had burritos or pizza, and yes, we had those as well. But Winston believed in his bagels, which he would serve piping hot with cream cheese and whatever other toppings you wished. He was a man ahead of his time and the lines for his bagel cart became legendary. Drunk students would spill directly out of whatever bar they had frequented and immediately know that they needed a quick bagel for the walk home. I myself have partaken of this genius's wonderfully fresh bagels at two in the morning, and I can vouch for their quality and helpful nature when it comes to hangover prevention. I have no idea where Winston is now, but in my imagination he is a very rich man drinking premium red wine as he stares at the rolling hills of his massive property, his fortune built on bagels sold to drunk college kids.

My parents live in the epicenter of the party zone. They live across the street from a particularly raucous party house that has been passed down from generation to generation of punk-rock partiers. As I went to sleep, I would often hear the late-night party howls of students stumbling home from this house or from the bars on The Strip as they made their way toward their apartments. I remember finding the noise oddly comforting. My own wife attended Southern Illinois

University for a brief spell. When she first met my parents, she charmed them with her great smile and personality and the nearly immediate confession that she believed she had more than once passed out on their lawn. Small world, right?

Southern Illinois University is also the home to many amazing festivals and celebrations (remember . . . party school). There is "Springfest" (a party in the spring, in which they get bands to play and have food and beer tents everywhere). There is "The Cardboard Boat Regatta" (a contest created by an SIU professor who challenged his students to create seaworthy vessels out of cardboard. It got very popular and became a yearly event during which cardboard vessels are raced around a pond by eager captains. I entered the contest when I was in high school with a boat that looked like the Led Zeppelin blimp. We did not finish the course). But the granddaddy of all parties at SIU has to be Halloween, and, well, you know what Halloween is. Except at Southern Illinois University, Halloween was a lot more than just your average dress-up-and-pass-out-candy-type thing.

On Halloween in Carbondale, The Strip would close off to cars and fill up instead with tens of thousands of college kids dressed in wild costumes. They were not sober, as you may have guessed. Folks came from hundreds of miles away to walk around in their C-3PO suits and pimp outfits and Michael Jackson costumes, drinking beer and partying down. Lots and lots of cheap beer was consumed. Later into the evening, the college kids would get really rowdy and do things like throw empty bottles of beer into the night sky. If you were underneath one of those bottles as they returned to earth, you were shit out of luck. The Halloween party was eventually shut down by the city after a group of drunk students set fire to a Ford Fiesta, a block away from my parents' house. What a buzz kill that was. It was fun while it lasted, though, that's for sure.

As a kid, I loved everything about Halloween. I loved the hustle and bustle, the young people with all their high-energy partying and having a blast. We were always right in the mix, too, getting dressed up and mingling with the crowd. One year, my dad dressed up as the Jolly Green Giant. He went shirtless, painting his face and body green. He then went walking up and down The Strip while carrying an axe that he'd also painted green. The cops agreed that it was a great costume but asked him to head home, as they didn't need a big green man walking around amidst a bunch of drunk college kids while carrying a real axe. Of course, Dad was offended.

The Halloween I am thinking of was the year I was thirteen. I had suddenly become very political. I was suddenly a very liberal boy. Maybe it was Reagan, or maybe because I liked rock and roll, which didn't feel conservative. Or maybe it was that I was turning thirteen and was beginning to sharpen my skills for the teen angst/acting-out bit. Whatever the reason, I had a brilliant idea for a costume. I would dress as a businessman, but that's not all. The kicker was the sign I planned to hang around my neck, which would state, "This is a Republican Asshole." I'll grant you that this was not my finest comedic moment, and it was unkind to be sure. At thirteen I was certainly unclear about what exactly a Republican might be, or the varying degrees of Republicanism. And I am sure that I was friends with people who were indeed Republicans, and it was certainly wrong to say that all Republicans are assholes. But I felt good about my costume decision at the time—in the way that a thirteen-year-old feels good about things.

I proudly dressed in my idea of business attire, which was a wide tie and a gray sweater-vest combo, then wrote the words on the placard and hung it around my neck. I waltzed into the living room to show my parents my brilliant idea.

"What do you think?" I asked.

My mom looked a bit north of uneasy, and my dad stared at me for a very long time. Neither of them said a word for what felt like an hour, but was probably only ten seconds.

"You look great, lad," my dad finally said. And off we

went, up and down The Strip, where I could be paraded in front of the tens of thousands of insanely drunk college students, many of which were presumably Republicans.

"Hon, are you sure?" my mom said as we walked out the door. It was 1986, a conservative time. SIU was a liberal campus, as many are, but Carbondale is surrounded by small towns that are much more conservative, and my mom was pretty sure we would find trouble.

"We'll be fine," my dad simply said.

My dad and I walked down The Strip together, keeping our eyes peeled for trouble. Mostly people liked my costume. I got plenty of "Hell yeah, little man!" Words cannot describe my pride during those moments. I had accomplished my goal of being a true, in-your-face liberal. And I enjoyed being the center of attention. But then we were stopped on the street. A big guy was suddenly standing in front of me, seemingly annoyed by my costume. He read the sign on my chest out loud, very slowly.

"This. Is. A. Republican. Asshole."

To this my pop simply replied, "Yup, that's what it says. Are you one?"

The guy seemed stunned at that one, and I thought I even saw him ball up his fist for a second. But then, he thought better of it and just walked away into the crush of people.

Later on that night, I saw the best costume I'd ever

———

seen in my thirteen years of life. Two incredibly tall guys were dressed as the bearded members of ZZ Top, complete with the long black trench coats. As I stood and stared at them for a bit, they yanked open their coats to reveal—you guessed it—the most gigantic fake dongs that have ever been created. The tip of each fake fabric penis literally dragged the sidewalk. Then one of them coolly said to us, "Happy Halloween," before both closed their

coats and went on to find their next victim. Maybe they weren't the most creative guys in the world, but man did they have panache. I was impressed.

When Halloween rolls around in our house, I'm pretty sure that whatever my daughters choose will not require me to dodge would-be attackers. If I'm honest, I probably wouldn't let my girls walk around a crowd with an aggressive sign as part of their costume. I'm not as cool a customer as my dad. But of course, I'll foster their beliefs and respect them when they start to sprout. I love that I was so into politics at that young of an age that I felt compelled to wear that costume— but what I love more is that my dad barely blinked an eye as we walked through that crowded street. He showed me that my opinions mattered.

Also, to be honest, I think he really agreed with the sign.

22

Learn the Rules of the Game

or Never Leg-Whip a Priest

MY WIFE REFERS TO my dad as "the most robust man on earth," which I think is a great description. One example of his robustness is his approach to exercise. He's always been a pretty fit and active guy. Back in the day he lifted weights, played tennis, and went on the walks he loves so much. But his favorite form of exercise has always been hoops. He's actually a pretty good player. He has a set shot that takes a while to prep, but once he lets the ball go, it's got a good chance of going in. He plays an old-school style of basketball, which suits him just fine. He's proud of his passing ability and would measure his day on the court by how many assists he got, and whether his team won, not how many times he got to dunk the ball. Which was never. If he played poorly, he would howl to the heavens, "Jesus Christ, Steve—that's not basketball!" or "Jesus Christ, Steve—you piece of shit!" Most of the time his rants would begin with "Jesus Christ, Steve," and the rest was sort of a fun Mad Lib in which he'd scream about how awful he was in some way or another. Or some-times he would scream about how awful he was in all ways. My brother and I are competitive too, of course, but my dad has the most volume, hands down.

As my brother got taller and better at basketball, often-times the games were Dad and me against Flynn. I think we won only about half the games we played against my brother (in our defense, he's really tall!). My dad played with my brother, our friends, and me for a long time, until he was in his early fifties. I retired from hoops long before Dad did. I retired at the age of forty-two, when I became aware that every time my friends and I played, we were risking serious injury. One friend tore his Achilles' heel and another thought he'd torn his ACL. One morning after a game, I woke up and couldn't move my leg. I went to see the knee doctor, who told me I had just sprained it and wouldn't need surgery. He then told me I should keep playing basketball, and that I'd be

———

fine. Then he told me that in full disclosure, he had torn his ACL playing basketball a year earlier. I had seen and heard enough. So I retired.

But long before I hung it up, I got to enjoy the basketball court across the street from our house that was installed by the Catholic church. I was about thirteen when this happened. It was a pretty big deal at the time.

Priests would come and go every few years through the Catholic church across the street, and word got out that Father Carl, the new priest, was a good basketball player. My brother, Dad, and I were always looking for a fourth, so we kept our eyes open for said Father. One day as we were playing, Father Carl, who was a fit guy in his fifties, popped out of his office to watch. Right away we asked him if he wanted to join the game. I mean, it was his court, after all. Well, Father Carl wasted no time whatsoever. He had a sweet, sure shot and was quick on his feet to boot. It was Father Carl and I matched up against Flynn and my dad. My brother had me overmatched, but Father Carl and I were hanging in there against Flynn and my dad. The reason, of course, is that Father Carl was eating my dad alive. Sweet mid-range jumpers. A real nice first step to the hoop. Dad was being outplayed in every way. Father Carl was wiping the court with my pop, and it wasn't pretty to watch. I could see my dad was trying as best he could to take it all in stride.

As we approached the end of the game, or "nut-cutting time" as my dad called it, the score was tight. My mom wandered out to our side porch and yelled out, "Hi, Father Carl!"

"Hi, Peg!" he answered, and they exchanged pleasantries about playing basketball and the lovely weather and other small talk, all while Father Carl continued to kick my dad's ass.

Now despite my mom's pleasant conversation with the Holy Father Carl, I should say that we were not a religious family. My mother grew up Lutheran and even attended a Lutheran college. My dad grew up Catholic and also went the religious route for school when it came to high school and college. Maybe after all that, they just decided enough was enough? I don't know, but I only ever went to church to play basketball. Mom and Dad describe themselves as spiritual, and so do I, though I do not share my father's fascination with St. Francis of Assisi. Take a look at this picture:

If you ignore the fact for a moment that he is

dressed like a lunatic Phillies fan, you might notice that he has two statues of St. Francis of Assisi flanking his fireplace. He has three or four more in his yard. I don't have lots of statues of saints in my yard, but I do believe in a higher power. When I take long walks with my daughters and Vivian asks me all about Jesus and Buddha, I answer as truthfully* as I can.

Once my mother stopped chatting with Father Carl, the game picked up in earnest. I had the ball. And I passed it to Father, waiting for him to make a move. He passed it back to me and I faked a shot, but my brother was right on top of me, so I passed it right back to Father Carl. Father Carl then took an explosive first step toward the hoop, blowing right past my dad, when my dad stuck out his knee and did the unthinkable. He. Tripped. The. Priest. That's right. He tripped Father Carl, who went down hard with a loud "Oomph!" as he hit the concrete. I didn't know how to react.

"Jeez, Dad!" my brother yelled.

"No, no. That's how we played where I grew up, too," Father Carl said as he slowly got to his feet. It looked like he was in pain, but he seemed very easygoing about the whole "leg-whip you to the ground thing" that my dad had just pulled on him.

---

* See chapter 4. Remember that sometimes I don't realize I am lying.

My mom was visibly embarrassed, and immediately ran over, saying, "Are you okay, Father Carl? Do you need some ice?"

"No, no," Father Carl said, and he thoughtfully rubbed his face, maybe wondering if he really did need some ice. "I'll be fine, thank you."

With that, my mother turned on her heel and went inside. She had seen enough.

The rest of the game was played in a completely non-physical way. I can't remember who won, but I do remember that we all shook hands in an over-the-top display of good sportsmanship. Father Carl's knee was a little bit bloody after my dad whacked him to the ground, but he was cheerful and gracious about the whole thing. I must note, however, that Father Carl never played with us again.

When speaking to my dad about the Father Carl incident, even to this day, he is surprisingly defiant. When pressed on the matter, my dad will say simply, "It's my lane."

What I've taken away from this is that no matter how badly I play, no matter what else I do, I will never leg-whip a priest. We never know which direction life will take us, but I am fairly confident that I will achieve this goal. My other takeaway is that I will always admire the strength of my father's convictions, however crazy they may be. I'll try to have a similar strength in my convictions, minus the craziness.

I mean, my dad really believes that in basketball, the lane belongs to the guy who is playing defense. If you come inside, whether you are a man of God or not, you are risking a big, hard foul that knocks you to the ground.

23

Always Support Your Children

Even When They Lose Their Way and Take Their Waiter Job Way Too Seriously

I MOVED TO LOS Angeles in 1995. I had earned my degree from the University of Illinois in Speech Communication. To this day, I have no idea what that degree prepared me for.

I chose to major in Speech Communication because it seemed like it wouldn't be too challenging, and I figured I liked to talk, so I could get good grades. I wasn't interested in anything like Pre-med or International Relations or the other

majors my friends might have been pursuing. I had no plans for a conventional career after college.

From a very young age, I was obsessed with comedy. I stayed up late watching stand-up comedy specials on HBO. I taped every episode of *Cheers* on our family VCR. In fact, I watched every sitcom on television. (In so doing, I discovered the erotic power of *WKRP in Cincinnati*. I was thirteen years old. This show featured Loni Anderson *and* Jan Smithers? Come on, it's impossible for a teenager not to masturbate to that show. Really, it's probably impossible for anyone. I dare you to try it.) I watched every funny movie that kids my age loved, *Caddyshack* and *Ghostbusters* and the like. I recognized early that Harold Ramis, Dan Aykroyd, Bill Murray, and John Hughes were seemingly a part of everything great out there. I watched every episode of *Saturday Night Live,* and was especially fascinated with Robin Williams and Eddie Murphy. My friends and I would listen to cassette tapes of their comedy shows on the way to soccer tournaments and we knew every single line. Our parents knew they were pretty dirty routines, but I think they all thought they were funny, too, so they let it slide. I would do some of Robin Williams's routines at my parents' parties and got a pretty good response, so that was good enough for me at an early age to decide on a career path. Comedy was the only thing that really made sense, because it was the only thing I felt like I might have a chance to be good at. I wanted to be a stand-up comedian, like George Carlin or Ellen DeGeneres or Richard Pryor or any other one of my heroes. I loved how they could give you an effortless peek into something so personal and make you laugh because you recognized the same horseshit in yourself. So really, I knew what I wanted to do. But I still figured I should go to college and get my degree. This was for two reasons:

1. Out of respect for my parents, who both had college degrees and valued what the degrees stood for. Also, they were paying.

2. I was scared to go to Los Angeles to pursue comedy, and this was a nice pit stop. I was scared that I'd fail, of course. I was scared of the idea of performing live for people, which didn't inhibit my desire to do it in the least. I told myself that if I could just make it into a place like The Second City, where so many of my heroes had started, that would be enough for me to call it a career. What came after that never even occurred to me.

I took most of my classes with football players, who were also there presumably for an easy path to good grades so they could stay on the team. I actually took classes with Simeon Rice, who went on to be a major NFL player who won a Super Bowl with the Tampa Bay Buccaneers and was chosen to the Pro Bowl three times. He once gave a gut-wrenching speech about some of the obstacles that he had to overcome on his way to college, and it was far and away the best speech that any of us ever gave and definitely better than anything I ever did.

I also started taking acting classes in college, and learned quite quickly that I was not equipped to major in Theater. I enjoyed improv classes and beginning acting classes, and have done all manner of silly trust exercises with other young actors, including sprinting with a blindfold on. I attempted to take an upper-level acting course and found myself in a dusty section of the Krannert Center for the Performing Arts at the University of Illinois, sitting with five thirty-eight-year-old classmates who in my memory all wore fedoras, and a gray-haired professor. I was nineteen, with an inside-out sweatshirt, a braided belt, and my hat on backwards. To say I did not fit in is an understatement. To open class, the professor told us all about opening up emotionally, and he began to tell a story of adopting his child and then he cried. And the five thirty-eight-year-olds wearing fedoras all cried. And I sat there thinking, "How quickly can I get the fuck out of here?" The answer was super quick.

I had a good time in college and it was the pit stop I was hoping for, and I like to think I learned a bit and matured a bit as well. I studied improv under a teacher I loved named Brian Posen, who made improv seem fun and The Second City seem like the Holy Grail. I trained at The Second City in Chicago for the summer of my junior year (Brian Posen had to convince them to let me into level one after I bombed the audition), and it opened my eyes to the idea that if I bombed out at stand-up, I could join a troupe and bomb consistently with other performers—which seemed like more fun anyway.

After I graduated, I moved back home with my parents in Carbondale for a few months and took a job at a Chinese buffet to save up the $2,000 that I felt was sufficient to give me a start in Los Angeles. What I remember most about that job is serving gigantic iced teas to people who were really, really thirsty. Like, novelty-sized iced teas. I guess if you're at an all-you-can-eat buffet, you want a super-big all-you-can-drink iced tea. Once a big guy who had to be six foot five or so, and seemed to be a farmer who'd just done some work in the sun, had me wait as I refilled his glass three times before he let me toddle off to give someone else their gigantic novelty tea. I was saving money, though, and I never forgot that I needed exactly $2,000 to get to LA. Why that was the amount never occurred to me. But I saved it up somehow (let's face it, my parents probably fronted me a grand—I wasn't making huge tips from the iced tea drinkers). Also at that time, I became very interested in karaoke and was probably still doing that damn comedic dancing at parties.

When the day came to leave to pursue my dreams in comedy, I drove my Saab (a gift from my dad, bought from the man who owned the tobacco shop in Carbondale), equipped with a CB radio that I bought from a pawnshop, all the way to Los Angeles. I had $2,000, bad skin, and a very limited skill set. *Let's do this!* My loose plan was to arrive in Los Angeles and roughly three days later join the cast of *Saturday Night Live*.

I traveled to LA in a two-car caravan with my funny friend Brian Tousey, who I'd met in college in my improv class and did sketch comedy with, and we kept ourselves occupied with those CB radios by giving ourselves endless new trucker names. If anyone else was on that channel, I'm sure they hated us with a white-hot heat.

When we got to LA, Brian and I stayed with my brother in a kind of rough section of Koreatown. This echoed how we'd stayed with my brother on the floor of his apartment in Chicago when we studied at The Second City (yes, Brian Tousey and I studied at Second City together as well. He did not bomb his audition). In LA, we slept on the floor and worked terrible temp jobs while we tried to figure out the comedy world. A gardener used to start his loud truck up at 5:30 in the morning every morning and fill our apartment with weird black smoke. A rough way to start your day. Brian and I finally got a small place on the west side of LA, made just enough money to make rent, and I began level one of The Groundlings. I quickly realized that stand-up was not my particular thing, and that I enjoyed the camaraderie that came with working in a group. I went my own way as I progressed in The Groundlings School, and made new friends who remain my best friends on earth today.

I tried not to complain about how hard the road was, as this was my choice, and I suppose I could have gotten a job as a professional speech-giver or something. It was impossible to find an agent. The first one I met worked in a one-room apartment and told me hopefully, "You look like a cop. You might be able to get some cop jobs," and then didn't sign me.

———

I waited tables and temped, and the jobs were not the ray of sunshine that one might hope for. I did a temp job in which I had to copy approximately 700,000 documents on a Xerox machine. When you loaded in the paper, it took maybe five minutes for it all to go through before the next load. I had a chair that was taken away, presumably because they thought sitting while the machine churned out the paper made me seem lazy. Through it all, my parents were very supportive and totally respected my decision to try to do something a bit out of the ordinary. Pursuing a career in comedy seems somehow less out of the ordinary now. Improv classes are offered everywhere, and thanks to the success of folks from The Groundlings, The Second City, and the Upright Citizens Brigade, many are familiar with the mechanics of making comedy and the path to a career in that world. These days, kids have seven careers by the time they are thirty-five, take sabbaticals and head to Tibet for a bit just because they feel like it, and make their first million in tech by twenty-eight. Don't they? I don't really know what the kids do, so I made that part up. But whatever it is today, it really wasn't that way in the '90s. Working a bunch of jobs while pursuing comedy was odd then, or at least for a kid from the Midwest. So, I have my parents to thank for not pushing me to take the more conventional path. Never once did they tell me that what I was doing might not actually turn out the way I hoped.

In order to survive in Los Angeles, I had to make my living the way millions of struggling performers before me (and after me) had done—by waiting tables. I worked for many different fine establishments, but my primary employer was the California Pizza Kitchen. For those who aren't familiar with it, California Pizza Kitchen is a restaurant chain that sells *wild and exciting pizzas for an affordable price!* BBQ chicken pizza—a game changer! Tostada pizza! Whaaaat? That sounds crazy, but it's soooo delicious! I first worked in the downtown Los Angeles location, after my friend Ronnie Repple from college put in a good word for me. Then I moved on to the Brentwood location, with the occasional stop at the Marina del Rey location. I barely made ends meet, selling Thai chicken pizzas to lawyers at lunchtime as I waited for my show-biz ship to come in. I needed to have my days free to audition, you see, even though I had no agent and no way to audition. One time I was approached by a producer of a television movie to audition for some sort of space-shuttle disaster miniseries and I got very sweaty, yelled all my lines, and was nicely and quickly told I did a great job as they gave the part to a much more deserving performer. That was my first audition and I was terrible. Wait—The Second City was my first audition and I was super terrible. At my Groundlings audition, I managed to pick at a pimple on my face and had to deliver a monologue as my face was bleeding. I was mortified beyond comprehension, but referenced the blood and Mindy Sterling, the hilarious actor, somehow must have thought that was good enough. Because other than the fact that I didn't run screaming out of the room in embarrassment because of my bloody face, I wasn't very good. She must have thought, "If this little maniac is willing to give it a shot with a bloody face, he at least deserves a chance to start the class." Thanks, Mindy. I owe you one. So as I bombed audition after audition and occasionally showed some sort of very loose definition of the word *potential*, I waited tables. I believe that my combined CPK time of service approached five years before I got very, very fired.

As the years went by, and I was more and more removed from the entertainment industry in which I could not gain traction, I got more and more sucked into my job at CPK in ways that didn't make sense. I started to lose track of who I was, what I was pursuing, and what the fuck I was doing in Los Angeles in the first place. What I mean is, I got *very* serious about my work at California Pizza Kitchen. I should preface this by saying that there is absolutely nothing wrong with waiting tables, and I came across many great people in my ten years doing that job, people who genuinely liked their jobs and were awesome at doing them. But I was waiting tables to make money as I pursued something else—my career in comedy. It was a means to an end. It wasn't the means itself, but I started to act like it was. I got frustrated when I didn't get a good section at work. I knew that I deserved the good tables and best shifts because dammit, I had earned that. I was competitive. I needed to be the best waiter in the place. I became a person who was probably not very much fun to work with. My apologies go out to the CPK Brentwood staff circa 1999.

I hit bottom on a trip home for Christmas in the year 1998. I had been in Los Angeles for three years and was well into "losing my way." I guess if I were interested in the restaurant business, I could have pursued restaurant management at that point. I'd put in the time. I was acting like this was my path, even though it wasn't. But I was not really doing much to further my acting career, either. I'd stumbled into a few auditions, not done great, and couldn't find an agent and didn't know what I'd do if I got one. I was going nowhere, basically. And barely making enough money to eat.

It was Christmas, and I was home in Illinois. I was so broke that for my mom's Christmas present, would you like to know what I got her? What did I get the woman who put me through college and supported my wild, crazy dream of a career in comedy? I gave her a California Pizza Kitchen cookbook. Because I could buy it at the restaurant with my employee discount. Shit, I'm still embarrassed about this. I gave her the cookbook and then I insisted that we make a Thai chicken pizza together.

Again, this is not embarrassing because I was ashamed to be working at this fine pizza establishment. Those Thai chicken pizzas are pretty tasty. It is mortifying to me because I had lost my way so completely. I had basically stopped trying to do what I really wanted to do, create a career in comedy, and had begun complaining about what it was I was actually doing, which was working at California Pizza Kitchen. Now I was trying to embrace what I was complaining about? I was truly a lost soul.

On Christmas morning, I presented my mother, who had done nothing but support me her whole life, with her incredibly lame gift. She simply smiled and said, "Oh, this looks like fun." Ever looking at the positive, my mother.

My dad crooked an eyebrow and just said, "Okay . . ." If one of my kids gave me such an obvious indication that she was losing her way, I would be very tempted to dive into a long lecture about choices and dreams and focus, which I'm sure she would promptly ignore. Dad, with his crooked eyebrow, did a lot more good. Sometimes, you say a lot more by saying less. Actually, my dad has only really given me hardline advice twice:

1. When I broke curfew with a friend when we were fifteen by walking around Carbondale to see what it was like at 3 a.m. His advice was, "That's when really bad people are around. That's stupid, son. Don't do it again." I listened.

2. When I got bad grades one semester in high school. This time his sage words were, "If you don't want to get stuck in this town or in a school you hate, you better get your shit together." I listened then, too.

My dad's advice usually was more along these lines:

- "Don't worry about that asshole. He has to be himself all day." (Though he would credit his good friend Joe Liberto for that one.)

- When I expressed concern over the fact that my dad was going to fly quite soon after the tragedy of 9/11, he gave me this gem: "Someone's gotta survive, and it's gonna be *me*."

- "Make sure you're doing well, son. If I were doing any better, I'd have to be twins." Gotta love that level of confidence. Especially when repeated every single day.

- "Watch where the huskies go and don't eat the yellow snow." (Not exactly original, but one of his favorites.)

- And finally, here is a little gem that he unveiled to me on the way to college: "When winter comes, and frost is on the punkin', that's the time for dickie dunkin'." I think my response at the time was something along the lines of, "Holy shit, Dad! Go easy." And he said, "What can I say, son? It's true."

After Christmas, I went back to Los Angeles and to my job at CPK. But soon after, something shifted in me. I realized that I needed to adjust my focus. I needed to remember why I had come to Los Angeles in the first place. I gave myself a very clear deadline to make some concrete decisions regarding my REAL career. I was moving through the system at The Groundlings; it's very much like a conservatory. There were four levels: Basic, Intermediate, Lab, and Advanced. After each level, you could either move ahead to the next level, repeat, or be asked to leave. I was completing my Advanced level, after which you were either asked to join the Sunday Company, which gives you a chance at becoming a Groundlings Main Company member, or you were asked to leave. I was doing nothing else of note, and was too serious about waiting tables and spending my money at bars after class instead of finding a way to make a dent with my career. So I told myself if I didn't make it into the Sunday Company I'd find something else to do with my life, maybe go to grad school and teach English lit? I imagined Portland as the place to do this, even though I'd never been there. In a stroke of amazing luck, I somehow made it into the Sunday Company. I firmly believe I was really on the bubble in this class, but sang a song that ended the show in which I basically asked The Groundlings (who would vote whether you stay or go) to let us all stay in. I did it to the tune of that Green Day song "Time of Your Life," and Melissa dyed my hair green and took the photos with me that made the slide show that accompanied the song. I basically begged for all of us to get into the Sunday Company and our teacher Mike McDonald, a superfunny and great actor as well as a great teacher back in the day, was crazy enough to let me try it. And I got into the Sun-

day Company on the strength of a maudlin song and a $1.99 bottle of green hairspray from Hollywood Toys & Costumes.

At around the same time that I was barely getting into the Sunday Company, I was unceremoniously fired from my waiter job via a bad "Secret Shopper" report. "Secret shoppers" are people that come into the restaurant and pretend to be customers. They grade you on your service. On this fateful night, the restaurant was very busy before the start of a movie at the theater nearby, and I got eight two-tops in my section in five minutes. The last table was my secret shoppers. I was tired, and over it, frankly. The secret shoppers graded me on how quickly I brought them their food and drinks, how knowledgeable I was regarding the menu, and my overall demeanor.

I got a 38 out of 100. I was slow to the table, got them their iced tea after the deadline, and told them that the shrimp scampi pizza was "really good"—vagueness was frowned upon by secret shoppers, who prefer words like "zesty!" or "a taste explosion!" I can only imagine that I lost the most overall points because my face was constantly trying to secretly tell the secret shoppers "please get me the fuck out of the California Pizza Kitchen." The company policy was to fire people in person, but when my manager called me I sniffed out the situation and asked for the dignity of being fired on the phone. He complied.

Being free of my waiter job meant that I had to really go for it as an actor. I was ready to really try. I'd met enough people with a strong work ethic and more sense than me (Melissa and others), so I had a better idea of what to do next. I'm lucky, because never once did my father bring down the hammer when I was struggling. He let me be a young dumb man in a big crazy city who was trying to figure it out. Both my parents let me make my own way, even during the brief time in my life when it looked like my way was a path to middle management at California Pizza Kitchen. My dad gave me constant encouragement about my real path, The Groundlings, and he took the waiting tables too seriously with a huge grain of salt. He was right.

Not giving constant unsolicited advice to my kids is going

to be very difficult for me, and I truly can make no guarantees to my kids that I will let them fly free. You see, I love to give long, boring speeches. Once in a while I will begin to orate on the importance of wearing sunscreen long after both of my children have already put buckets of it on. I can only imagine the temptation that will beckon me when they begin to explore their careers. Maybe on those occasions, when the temptation is just too much, I should go back to my secret hideout in Key West.

24

Teach Your Children the Value of Money

Spend It Now

MY DAD HAS ALWAYS been great with money. By this I mean he has always been free and easy with it. Money doesn't mean much to him. To his way of thinking, money is not nearly as important as what you can do with it, what you can get for it. For instance, when I was a kid, he used to give me money to clean out his pipes. He was a pipe smoker for a time, so I got one dollar per pipe I cleaned.

This was a strange and kind of gross job, and I don't blame him for not wanting to do it. Being a kid, I was game, because hey—a dollar a pipe was worth it. When I finished cleaning them, he would give me the money and say, "Spend this quickly. The government could change hands." Every single time this is what he said. And, like most kids, it was never a problem for me to spend all the money as quickly as possible, because it burned a hole in my pocket until I could go out and buy comic books and Dungeons & Dragons modules, which probably explains why I didn't have sex until much later in life.

Back in the day we would spend the summers in Ocean City, New Jersey, with Joe Liberto's family and other friends from Carbondale. By "summers" I mean for one week each summer, we'd all rent a big house close to the beach. On the Jersey shore there is the beach, of course, but so much more. There is great pizza, and snow cones, but also a boardwalk with tons of other kids to play with and an arcade! To me it was heaven. When we were at the shore, my parents were very generous. My dad would give me $20 in quarters a night and say, "Go crazy." And crazy I went, playing PAC-MAN, Galaga (I am quite certain that somewhere in a dirty arcade in Ocean City, New Jersey, I still have the eighth highest score ever. In my excitement I missed the *n* and entered "Beb"), and pinball and buying candy and all the rest. When I would come back later for more quarters, if he had more, he would give them to me, no questions asked. Never once did he chastise me for spending the $20 worth too fast. But if he was out of quarters, it was likely because my brother, or the kids of my parents' friends, had gotten to him first. Everyone knew he was a light touch.

My dad has always been generous this way. He gave me money. He gave my brother money. He gave my uncle money when he needed it. And it was always cash whenever possible, because my dad understood that cash is more fun than checks, especially when you are a kid. Every time that he'd come to visit me in college, he'd grab me in a bear hug when it was time to leave and pass me a $100 bill. I'd say thank-you and he'd always say something along the lines of "Spend it foolishly." And, oh, did I follow his advice! I ask you—when are you in a better position to spend money foolishly than when you're in college?

In the dark early days in Los Angeles, I found myself really needing my dad's help. I was living with Brian Tousey in West LA, I had lost my job at the California Pizza Kitchen, and the $400 a week that I had grown accustomed to was no longer coming in. I had been living off a credit card for a while. I put my Groundlings classes on my credit card, I got a cash advance from my card so I could pay my rent, and then I bought groceries with it, too. (In retrospect, the only worthwhile investment I made in those early dumb days was taking classes at The Groundlings. I felt at home there, I had friends there, and there was a new girl that I had a crush on who I eventually married.) On and on I went like this until one day I realized I was over $20,000 in debt. This freaked me out, big time. I felt like there was no way I would ever pay this debt back in my lifetime, especially given how my career was going. I couldn't get another restaurant job; apparently scoring 38 out of 100 on a "Secret Shopper" report is not too enticing for future employers. I did score a short-lived run as a waiter at Hamburger Hamlet, which was, to put it mildly, an emotional low. I made about $18 a shift and discovered that old people like to order their burgers very rare. So rare the kitchen staff didn't feel comfortable serving it at that temperature, so every day these barely cooked burgers went back and forth from the table (*"This is overcooked!"*) to the kitchen (*"I can't serve it this rare!"*) in a hopeless cycle of depression. One day I believe I waited on Neil Simon. I think he ate there all the time. He understood the minimum temperature the kitchen would send him his burger at, so I believe I was spared that *"this burger is too cooked"* dance one time by the old master.

Since I couldn't make any money whatsoever, I consolidated all of my debt into one big sum, through one of those debt consolidation loans. My payment was just over $300 a month. I quickly realized I didn't have that kind of cabbage and I had to come clean about the whole situation to my dad. To my dad's credit, during these years when he knew I was struggling, he would always ask me during our conversations, "How you doing for money?" I didn't have to hide that I was broke, and he didn't want me to have to go through the embarrassing process of continually asking him and my mom for money. My dad was generally aware of my horrible monetary situation, but this was a particularly low point. So when I laid it all out for him, my dad said, "You know what? I'll cover it."

"Jeez, Dad. That's nice." I was really touched. My dad was generous, but this was a time that his help meant more than just slipping me a few bucks for fun money. My pop covered that $300 payment for over a year. Probably two or three years. When I finally started to get some acting work I took over the payments again, and eventually paid off the debt in full. For years I've been offering to pay my dad back and he always just says, "Nah. That's all over, buddy." What a guy!

My kids have no idea what value money actually has. They believe that you can buy a car for anywhere from $1 to $100, which is of course crazy unless it's the Road Warrior.

Fuck you, Road Warrior, you evil beast! Burn in hell! Who am I kidding? I am sure that you are in a place of honor in hell, and Satan himself drives you to his various appointments when he is not busy changing your horrible, evil oil. But I digress. I'm still not over that car.

One day, my kids will both have to get jobs when they're old enough and want actual money to get actual stuff that they actually want, just like I did. And I hope they can adopt my dad's attitude about money, because the older I get, the more I am convinced that he's right. Sure, money is important, and it's important to save it and all that. Money is also just weird green paper that you can get stuff with. If you have a lot of money, you should try and help other people who don't have enough. And if you have enough of it, try to enjoy it. Treat yourself to a really nice glass of wine now and then.

When I was in my late twenties, my dad sent me this note:

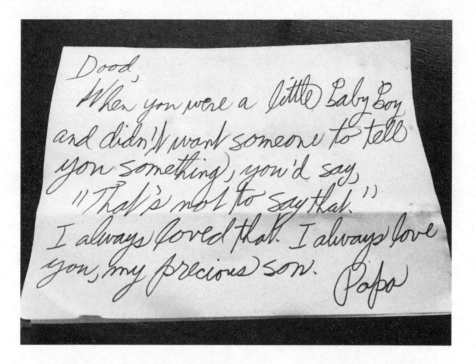

The note was wrapped around two crisp $100 bills. I spent the money, but I still keep the note in my desk. Some things—really most things—are much more valuable than money. My dad taught me that, too.

25

Find a Good Lady to Spend Your Life With

but Be a Good Husband

THERE IS A SAYING that the best way to be a good father to your children is to love their mother. I like to look at it this way: one of the best ways to be a good dad is to find a great lady to be the kids' mom. If you have a great wife who is a great mother, you have to keep up, as a husband and a dad. You can't slack off. You have to keep up. Melissa

---

is such a good person that I feel compelled to try my best to keep up.

My own mom is a great lady. She is kind and smart and has a strong backbone and a strong character. She doesn't worry too much about things that she cannot control. She likes good people and having fun with her friends. She loves her children and her grandchildren. Once in a while, she gets a little loopy and wears a sombrero or takes a swim in her basement. She spent her career trying to help people and to discern which people would do the most good with the resources she was able to get. This career path has made her an authority figure and someone with impeccable judgment. Someone whose opinion matters. My dad adores my mom and he recognizes that she is a truly good person, which is what he correctly values most in the world. She makes him a better person and he delights in trying to make her laugh and in trying to make every day a fun factory. He tells constant jokes and finds chocolate that they both might enjoy and consistently suggests that they drink champagne for lunch. So they're a good match indeed.

Like my dad, I have found a great lady. My wife is a really funny person and a good actor who has gone on to do well in movies. She's kind, pretty, and chatty, and she is prone to roller-coaster rides of emotion. I am boring and steady, so I balance her out. I often think of my wife as a force of nature, which I think is fairly accurate. Melissa has helped me to grow up and to understand (at least partially) what it means to be a gracious adult. For example, let's send a thank-you note, guys! It's easy and it's good manners. Melissa through her example helps me to remember to do the little things every day to try to make friends, family, employers, and employees feel appreciated and recognized, to feel heard. To make folks understand that they're important to you sometimes takes a bit of effort, but it's worth it. And it's right. My mom has helped my dad try and understand the same things. And when he is not falling asleep with chocolate pretzels in his pocket, he is mostly succeeding. I try to be a good husband, as I know my father has. I am sure that some days I do better than other days, but I follow the same two rules in being a husband that I follow in fatherhood. I show up, and I love my wife. I'm better when I keep things simple.

When Melissa and I met, she sat to the right of me in Level 3 of The Groundlings. It was a writing class in a back area of the Green Room. I felt immediately at home with her, like we'd known each other forever. Which in some ways, maybe we had. I was a simple kid from the Midwest, and she was an adult. I mean, she read books and took baths. In her own apartment, with no roommates! She had everything figured out, as far as I was concerned. I am prone to nervousness and immediately she made me feel like everything would be okay. She's also hot stuff and funny as hell, so quite a combo there.

When we get the girls ready for school, Melissa combs their hair and picks out nice clothes for them to wear. I make the girls bagels or gluten-free pancakes for breakfast, and I tell them wild stories of young powerful women who defeat evil forces while Melissa simultaneously tries to get them to put on their socks or brush their teeth. It's a chaotic, fun time, the mornings—and I'm so glad that she and I get to share our lives and our children together. Left to my own devices, the girls would go to school fed but sockless. When Melissa had to get to work early last week, that meant that I was in charge of getting them ready for school, solo-style. What that evolved into was an eventual fact that Georgie wore two different shoes to school. I didn't have the energy to win the battle that fateful morning without Melissa in my corner. We are a team, and it is the best way I can imagine living my life. We are doing our best to raise two extremely great girls, and I personally am happy as a clam about all of it. Though I have never understood why clams were happy. So I'll just say I'm happy.

This photograph was taken at our friends' house on a recent Halloween.

We trick-or-treated. The girls, as you can see, did not wear costumes that included the word *asshole* prominently featured upon them. The girls scored lots of candy, which I sorted through very carefully looking for razor blades and

other dangerous foreign objects (my dad would definitely eat the chocolate first and ask questions later). Melissa and I had a blast that day, with our girls, our friends, and our friends' kids. We've created our own version of the Carbondale gang, just like my parents had. We don't have The Pinch Penny Pub. But like my dad, I found a great lady to spend my life with who makes every day better.

Good times indeed.

26

Appreciate Every Gesture

For Example, the Meal That My Daughters Made Me for Father's Day, 2014

O NE TIME WHEN I was a kid, I wrapped up one of my Matchbox cars and gave it to my dad as a "present." I don't recall the occasion—his birthday, Father's Day, Christmas, could have been any of them. My dad never mentioned that I had just wrapped up one of my toys and handed it off to him. Instead, he was delighted to receive it, and we played with it together for a while. He even gave it back to me later when I asked for it.

This moment with my pop taught me to just enjoy the gifts your kids give you, no matter what they may be. He didn't care why I gave it to him. He just appreciated that I wanted to give him a gift. When I went to the kitchen on Father's Day and found an odd presentation, a breakfast that my girls were really proud of, I hesitated for a heartbeat, and then dove right in like I had been given a plate of eggs Benedict and a giant mimosa. And you know what? Once I got past the weird phallic presentation, this breakfast tasted pretty delicious— because my kids had made it for me with love. Also, almond butter with a banana is a pretty classic combination.

Luckily, however, they didn't ask for it back.

27

It's Okay to Cry

or The Art of Gathering Wine

DESPITE THE FACT THAT my father is a man with a big heart and strong emotions, he is not someone who cries often. He is not the steely manly man who is averse to crying, but he reserves crying for the saddest, most painful moments of life.

The last time I saw my father cry was when his mother, Marie Falcone, died. She was worth many tears, because she was a wonderful lady. I remember that she once called me in my dark days in Los Angeles. I think I was in my late twenties, and it was a year or two before she died. Out of the blue, my grandmother gave me literally the world's greatest pep talk. She spoke about how life can seem tough, but she believed in me. She told me that she hoped that I'd be happy no matter what happened in my life or career because she thought I deserved to be happy. She said to me, "You deserve to be happy because you're a good person, and that's the most important thing." Then she told me about a television show called *Falcone* and how I should try out for it. There was indeed a show on TV called *Falcone* for a season or so, but I was too embarrassed to call and say, "Hey, my last name is Falcone, so I should probably audition for a role somehow." And she was right—I should have called to at least try. I think I was pretty deeply in my "serious waiter" phase at that point.

I stammered through the rest of our phone call, thanking my grandmother profusely for her support. She was one of the all-time greats in life. She was an Irish mother in a house full of six boys, and she worried about every single member of her family.

My dad cried when she died, and while there's no shame in crying, there should be shame in *not* crying when a lady like my grandma passes away.

There was a traditional Catholic funeral and we went out for dinner afterward somewhere in Philadelphia, which is a city that morphs for me. I've been there so many times and yet I still never know exactly where I am. It's as though I pick up my dad's terrible sense of direction whenever we are in his hometown. To me, Philly is just a sea of good Italian restaurants—and there is nothing whatsoever wrong with that.

So my dad, my brother, two of my dad's brothers (remember, my Uncle Nick wasn't there because he disappeared into thin air), and aunts and cousins and great-aunts and great-uncles were gathered around a large table. My dad was in a quiet kind of mood, which unnerves me when it happens because as is abundantly clear by now he's one of the world's great conversationalists. I was sitting to my dad's right, my brother to his left. We were all drinking red wine. Normally my dad drinks white wine (he can just *fuck up* a bottle of chardonnay), but the occasion seemed to call for the solemnity of a red. I started to tell my dad a story about my grandma, his mom. It might have even been about the thoughtful pep talk she gave me all those years before. I honestly don't remember what I was telling him.

Whatever I was telling him must have registered with him in some form or fashion, because he looked at me with a tired, sad look and said, "I'd toast you, son, but you have no wine."

I politely informed him that he had my glass of wine in front of him, as well as his own. Then my brother turned to him and said, "You also seem to have my wine, Pop." My father looked down distractedly and said, "Ah, it appears that I do." My dad had indeed also gathered my brother's wine. In front of him were three glasses of red wine. He made no move to give any of it back, either. He just stared wistfully in front of him.

My Great-Aunt Helen peered down at us through the glasses on the end of her nose and said, "Ben, you look just like your grandfather. You have the Falcone nose."

"Thank you, Aunt Helen." I took it as a compliment.

My dad then turned to his brothers, Kevin and Gene.

"Let's raise a glass to Mom, Marie Falcone."

Flynn and I silently and swiftly slid our wineglasses away from Dad, and raised them for the exceptional woman who had raised our exceptional father.

What I learned that night is this: *If you are grief-stricken, it is acceptable to gather all of your children's wine.*

I would have let him keep it, too, but I had to toast my grandma.

Rest in peace, Marie Falcone. Thanks for everything, especially raising my father to be such a great man.

PS: As I write this, time inevitably passes. We lost my nice

Uncle Kevin several years ago and unfortunately we quite recently lost my Uncle Gene, who was a Vietnam veteran, firefighter, and all-around great guy. My dad is now the last living Falcone brother (we think). Here's to you, Uncle Gene, and to all the brothers, and to the children that you raised.

Gather your wine, indeed.

28

Choose Happy,

and It Is a Choice

THE ONE THING MY father has told me most in my life, the mantra he has repeated to me time and time again, is this: "Be happy." That seems like simple advice, doesn't it? Of course it is. And you know what? It is sometimes very difficult to achieve.

It was easy to be happy when I was a ten-year-old kid and my family was hiking in Giant City State Park. Flynn and I were pretending to be characters from *The Lord of the Rings* that day. We read those books at very young ages many times

---

over and became fanatical about them after my mom and dad casually mentioned that we might like them. I was being Gimli the Dwarf and Flynn was Legolas the Elf. We were running around the rocky terrain, and Flynn was really getting some air off some big rocks as we attacked invisible Orcs. My dad kept saying, "Slow down, guys," to which Flynn replied, "Fear not, I am Legolas the Elf."

On Flynn's next big jump my dad rolled his eyes and said, "Well, just don't break your elven ass."

We all laughed. It was a happy day.

It was easy to be happy when I got my soapbox race car for Christmas. It was a homemade, kid-sized car made out of wood. My mom and dad had a friend make it for me, and it was amazing. It was blue and beautiful, literally a work of art that was also a kid's toy, made by a kind man with a great name, Alan Harasimowicz. This was the best present ever. There were ropes attached to the inside of the car that made the axle turn the wheels. To make the wheels go left you actually had to turn the wheel right, which for a kid is not exactly easy to get used to, but it's easy to be happy when you and your dad are barreling down a hill and turning the wrong way into a bank of snow.

It was easy to be happy when, after a tornado leveled a huge tree in our front yard, my dad paid guys to cut it up and haul it away but had them cut the base of the tree into a giant throne. For months, Flynn and I would sit on our giant oak throne and survey our land. We were probably still pretending to be dwarves and elves. It is easy to be happy when you have parents who foster creativity and imagination in your life. It is easy to be happy when you have a childhood that lets you be a kid. So many kids today have to grow up way too fast. I know how lucky I was.

It is easy to be happy when you have a dad who lets you ride your bike next to him while he jogs. And doesn't get mad at you when he gets tired and you say, "You know, Dad, a real jogger wouldn't need to stop now." Supposedly I said that once, and my dad got up and jogged the rest of the way home. Those were happy times, when my dad appreciated my smart-ass remarks.

Christmases were happy, Thanksgivings were happy, Easters were happy—even after both the major and minor characters from these holidays had been revealed to be fictitious. Weekends were happy with soccer games, and Sunday nights at The Pinch Penny Pub. Friends and family and neighbors all made us happy. Good times and great friends. Almost always, in my childhood, it was easy to be happy.

In times that were less happy in life, my dad made me realize that sometimes being happy takes hard work. When you feel like shit, it takes effort to muscle through. "Everything happens fast, boy-o," he says. "Might as well enjoy it." He says, "I've enjoyed every part of my life more than the last." And he damn well means it. He's a guy who knows who he is, what he likes, and how to be good to other people.

And if there's a whole lot more to life than that, I'll eat a live turtle.

Being happy is a choice. It is a choice my father has made. It is the right choice, and I try every day to do the same thing. I'm going to teach my kids the same thing. Because my dad is right: "Life is short; you might as well try and enjoy it."

So here's to you, Mom, Dad, and Flynn. And Pop, I love you. Your happiness is contagious. Thank you for being you. Thank you for everything.

ACKNOWLEDGMENTS

I WANT TO THANK Carrie Thornton for editing this book and helping me to structure my thoughts (so often they tend to run around on their own), as well as for being such a nice person.

To Carrie's right hand, Sean Newcott. Since Carrie is my right hand, and Sean is Carrie's right hand—that makes Sean my *third* right hand. Which is cool.

Christian Donatelli, our manager and friend, who early on thought this book might actually be interesting or fun.

Simon Green, my agent—for helping me land on my feet with Carrie and HarperCollins.

The whole team at HarperCollins, for taking a chance on

me and believing in the book—and all of their excellent hard work that followed.

Liz Cohen, for putting together the first version of the book that I gave to my folks as a gift for Christmas.

Divya D'Souza for her relentless efforts proofreading, finding pictures, and coordinating elements of the book with my family, as well as good thoughts on improvements.

Melissa McCarthy, for being hot stuff and for writing the forward.

To the family friends, too numerous to mention, who made growing up in Carbondale in the Eighties such a special affair.

To my friends Steve and Lisa Mallory and the rest of the group now in Los Angeles—I hope and believe that all of our kids will remember growing up in the 2010s as a special and happy affair.

BEN FALCONE is a film director, writer, and actor. He has appeared in the films *Bridesmaids, Identity Thief,* and *The Heat,* and co-starred in *What to Expect When You're Expecting* and *Enough Said.* He wrote and directed the comedies *Tammy, The Boss,* and the upcoming *Life of the Party.* He is married to Melissa McCarthy and is the father of two daughters.